THE MEASURE
OF OUR DAYS

THE MEASURE OF OUR DAYS

WRITINGS OF
WILLIAM F. WINTER

EDITED BY

ANDREW P. MULLINS, JR.

Published by William Winter Institute for
Racial Reconciliation, University of Mississippi

Distributed by University Press of Mississippi

www.upress.state.ms.us

The University Press of Mississippi is a member
of the Association of American University Presses.

First edition 2006
∞

Library of Congress Cataloging-in-Publication Data

Winter, William F.
The measure of our days : writings of William F. Winter /
edited by Andrew P. Mullins, Jr.—1st ed.
    p. cm.
  ISBN-13: 978-1-57806-914-9 (cloth : alk. paper)
  ISBN-10: 1-57806-914-9 (cloth : alk. paper) 1. Mississippi—
Politics and government—1951- 2. Southern States—Politics
and government—1951- 3. United States—Politics and
government—Philosophy. I. Mullins, Andrew P., 1948–II.
Title.

F345.3.W56A25 2006
976.2′063—dc22   2006008333

British Library Cataloging-in-Publication Data available

CONTENTS

PREFACE

In January 2003, several of us at the University of Mississippi were preparing for a grand celebration of Governor William Winter's eightieth birthday. This function was being sponsored by the Institute for Racial Reconciliation which Winter had been instrumental in founding at the University. We planned to name the institute in his honor and announce the official designation at his birthday celebration in the Old Capitol Building in Jackson, Mississippi. I asked Governor Winter to provide some of the speeches he had made during his long involvement with racial reconciliation, so that I could select some quotations to go in the event's program. Moved by the eloquence, poignancy, and pragmatism found in his words, I asked to see more speeches on other topics.

During his six decades of public service and involvement, Governor Winter often delivered speeches extemporaneously. Those of us associated with him during his career believed that there was no record of his speeches or a very scattered collection at best. However, what we did know then, and what has remained true throughout his life, is that he never used a speech writer. Every speech he has made regardless of the issue or the occasion has been written by him.

For the last two years, I have read over four hundred speeches, lectures, commentaries, articles, and personal musings found in two large filing cabinets in Governor Winter's law office and in over one hundred boxes of his personal papers in the William F. Winter Archives and History Building. From these writings and from numerous interviews I conducted with him for my 1992 book, *Building Consensus, A History of the Passage of the Mississippi Education Reform Act of 1982*, I have identified many topics that he has eloquently addressed. I have taken excerpts from his various works and arranged them under these topics. Political speeches have been purposefully omitted. In fact his best speeches and writings have occurred in the last twenty years since his final political race. Unencumbered by politics, he has been able to speak freely on issues about which he feels strongly. However, I have included a few excerpts from his early speeches delivered during the turbulent 1960s to illustrate the progressive views Winter held on the difficult issues of that decade. Some of these speeches are truly remarkable considering the time and the context in which they were delivered.

If known, I have identified the date of the work, the title of the piece, and the place where it was delivered.

Throughout his writings consistent themes emerge—his commitment to a workable social contract, his belief in the value of every citizen, and his deep and abiding love for Mississippi. He is greatly loved and respected by many citizens of this state and region. He is disliked and reviled by some as well—primarily because of his long-term advocacy for racial reconciliation and for progressive public education and all of the controversy associated with those two volatile issues. He has never shied away from controversy regardless of its effects on the opinions his fellow Mississippians might have of him. Many of the topics covered in this publication will attest to that fact. However, he has no rancor in his heart whatsoever for those who have vehemently disagreed with his beliefs through the years. He treats everyone with respect and has always given differing opinions a respectable hearing. Winter is remarkable in his ability to separate the message from the messenger and to disassociate his disagreement with a person's opinion from a dislike of the person—a sign of a statesman.

In a recent edition of the *Washington Post*, nationally syndicated columnist, David Broder, said, "All of us have people we can turn to when we're in need of inspiration. For many years, one such person in my life has been former Mississippi Governor, William Winter, a man whose courage and leadership, especially on racial and educational issues, have been demonstrated for decades."

William Winter often speaks the truth as he sees it in poetic fashion in hopes of advancing his beloved state and its citizens on the issues he views as most important. As a leader he has given his opinions on what is best for Mississippi, the South, and the nation above the fray of partisan politics—the dictionary definition of a statesman.

The noted author, David Halberstam, called William Winter his favorite politician and personal hero. In his dedication address for the William F. Winter Archives and History Building on November 7, 2003, Halberstam said:

> I believed for a long time that America would not be whole until
> Mississippi became part of it, and you [Winter] more than any
> other politician are the architect of the new Mississippi and the
> new America. . . . What made you special as a politician was in
> the end something elemental in all our best politicians—a faith in
> the nobility of ordinary people, and a belief that if spoken to with
> candor and decency, they can rise to the occasion. It is nothing
> less than the most basic premise of a working democracy. Have
> faith in the people and their better nature. You understood the
> importance in this state, of the special burden of the past, and the
> responsibility to the future and again and again in your decisions,

blended mercy and compassion and a sense of justice against the harsher pressures of immediate political necessities. You were both educator and governor. These are not abstract choices I am talking about. They are real and they are immediate and they are always with us. As we respond to those choices we define ourselves, often in ways we don't really understand. And not everyone behaves as well as Governor Winter.

The selections in this book serve as the testimony of one of Mississippi's finest statesmen—one who has served and continues to serve his state, region, and country for over sixty years. His outstanding service to both public and private entities has been extraordinary since he first entered the armed services in 1943. This publication embodies his wisdom and his remarkable contributions.

—ANDREW P. MULLINS, JR.

INTRODUCTION

William Forrest Winter was born on February 21, 1923, in the small town of Grenada roughly ten miles from his family's farm in Grenada County, Mississippi. His great-grandfather, William Hooe Winter, Jr., migrated to Mississippi from Charles County, Maryland, through Alabama to the Yalobusha River wilderness. This land had been ceded by the Choctaw Indians in the Treaty of Dancing Rabbit Creek.

His maternal great-grandfather, Ephraim S. Fisher, came to this same Mississippi frontier from Kentucky where at Centre College he had received a law degree. The Fisher and Winter farms adjoined along the Yalobusha River. Fisher had a successful law practice and became a member of the Mississippi Supreme Court. He was also an outspoken Whig and an opponent of secession.

William Hooe Winter's son, William Brown Winter, served under General Nathan Bedford Forrest during the last years of the Civil War and later would recount his war experiences to his grandson whose middle name, Forrest, was in honor of his commanding officer. After the war, William Brown married Judge Fisher's daughter, Amelia, and settled on the family land in Grenada County.

William Forrest Winter in the lap of his grandfather William Brown Winter.

This union yielded four children but only one survived— William Aylmer Winter, who was born in 1872. He was reared on the farm in Grenada County, but the family later moved to Grenada to be close to a school so their son could complete his education. He graduated from high school and subsequently completed Iuka Norman Institute where he graduated first in his class at age nineteen.

William Aylmer Winter taught school for a few years and then became a farmer and cotton buyer and was elected to the state legislature in 1915. In 1921 he married a schoolteacher, Inez Parker, from the Calhoun County community of Big Creek.

They lived in a modest house built by his father on the family farm. Into this environment the only child of William Aylmer Winter and Inez Parker Winter was born. In his unpublished memoir William Forrest Winter describes his rural world: "It was a way of life closer to that of the nineteenth century than the twentieth. It was the setting that formed the basis of my earliest memories, that marked my childhood and did much to shape my personal values and my later political ideals. It was in William Faulkner's words my 'postage stamp' of family and place and time and events that, as for all of us for better or worse, form the unique character of our lives."

At age five Winter became his mother's informal student in a school established in a storage shed on the family farm. Both of his educated parents were diligent in the education of their only child. The seeds of Winter's enduring support for education were planted in these early experiences in the former cottonseed shed school. His elementary education continued in a one-room public school called Kincannon which was named for Andrew Kincannon, a former University of Mississippi chancellor and State Superintendent of Education. He would complete his elementary and high school education in Grenada.

Many of Winter's childhood friends and playmates both black and white came from the sharecroppers on the family farm and from neighboring farms. He was one of a very few to complete high school. This situation had a profound effect on him. At an early age he recognized the limits placed on the education of the black children, and he would later refer to the hard conditions many of his friends faced due to their lack of formal education. His fortuitous upbringing by two educated parents in comparison to his peers greatly influenced him and led to his deep passion for public education.

Winter's father subscribed to several newspapers and magazines and the family had a battery powered radio—there was no electricity in the house during his entire childhood—to connect

Nine-year-old William Winter with his father, State Senator William
Aylmer Winter, 1932.

to the outside world. His father was a well-read man and did all
in his power to make sure his son benefitted from a variety of
educational experiences including travels around the state.

One trip of special significance was taken in 1932. Winter,
age nine, accompanied his father who was a state senator at the
time to Jackson on the train from Grenada to attend the inau-
guration of Governor Mike Conner. All of the ceremonies sur-
rounding that event in the capital city made a deep impression
on the young Winter, who met the newly inaugurated governor in his office in the Mississippi capitol building. Winter later
wrote in his memoirs the description of this occasion:

> The governor shook my hand, led me behind his huge desk, and
> sat me in his chair. My legs were barely long enough to hang over

the edge of the seat. I could not see over the desk. He looked at
me and grinned. "That chair just fits him," he said to my father,
who winked at me across the room. At that moment I could
think only of what I was going to tell the boys back home. Most
of them didn't know who Mike Conner was. The parents of my
white friends had been mostly for Bilbo. The parents of my black
friends couldn't vote at all. But I was impressed that the newly
inaugurated governor would take the time to shake my hand and
let me sit in his big chair.

Winter continued to visit his father at the Capitol for the next
several years. He found the legislative process very intriguing
and entertaining; he became fascinated with the debates, the
issues, the history, and the characters involved in state government. His father was his hero and was never defeated in six
terms in the legislature.

Winter graduated from Grenada High School in 1940 as vale-
dictorian of his class of fifty-two and passed up an academic
scholarship offer from Millsaps College in Jackson to enter the
University of Mississippi in the fall of that year. From the beginning of his days in higher education, Winter showed signs of
strong leadership abilities.

In his freshman year, he immediately became involved in
one of his great loves—journalism. He joined the staff of the student newspaper, *The Mississippian*, which was published once
a week. He was the sportswriter, a role which he "took very
seriously," modeling himself after Walter Stewart, the famous
sportswriter for the *Commercial Appeal*. He later became the
editor of the student newspaper and has continued a lifelong
passion for good journalism including sportswriting.

As a freshman he was on the honor roll and involved in his
fraternity, Phi Delta Theta. The Cardinal Club, a student service organization, named him the outstanding freshman for the
1940–41 academic year. In his junior year, he was selected to

Omicron Delta Kappa, which recognizes outstanding leadership. Winter graduated after three years with a double major in political science and history and a minor in English. After military training he came back to Ole Miss in 1944 for a brief time and took additional courses while remaining with his ROTC class. He was then one of six chosen for the Ole Miss Hall of Fame.

Winter credits his teachers at Ole Miss with expanding his intellectual horizons and introducing him to a less provincial world. Of special importance to him were the popular and respected professor of political science, Huey B. Howerton, and the distinguished historian and author of *Mississippi: The Closed Society*, James Silver. He and the controversial Silver were friends for many years and corresponded on political matters for over twenty years after Winter's graduation. In 1950 when Winter was a young first term legislator he defended attacks on Silver by some of his legislative colleagues who had introduced legislation termed the "Subversive Act of 1950." Silver was one of five at Ole Miss labeled as "undesirable professors" for their "liberalism" and for their hosting nationally known speakers with "biased political lines of thought." Winter publicly took the floor of the House of Representatives to defend the teaching staff, specifically Jim Silver and to defend ODK at the University of Mississippi as the sponsoring organization for these controversial speakers.

During the summer of 1941 after his freshman year, Winter worked for the Department of Agriculture measuring crop acreage. This job was part of the New Deal program to stabilize cotton prices by limiting the amount of cotton that was planted. The work entailed visiting the farms in Grenada County and surveying the planted fields. He got to know the cotton farmers well and came to know what it took to survive as a small cotton farmer. Many of these farmers whom he met that summer became lifelong friends and later some of his most loyal political allies.

As World War II raged, Winter's ROTC class remained intact during the academic year of 1942–43. Many of his friends and classmates were already casualties by this stage of the war. The day after graduation in 1943 the Ole Miss ROTC class was ordered to report to Camp Blanding in Florida for seventeen weeks of basic infantry training. In April 1944 Winter reported to the infantry officer candidate school at Fort Benning, Georgia.

Here Winter had his introduction to official racial integration when a black soldier was assigned a bunk next to his. He and other candidates from the South developed a close camaraderie with the African American officer trainees. As Winter later said, "We found that we spoke the same language and supported each other."

In October 1944, seventy-one candidates out of a starting contingent of 210 qualified to become second lieutenants. Winter graduated first in the class and fully expected to be assigned to a combat division. Instead he was ordered to report to the Infantry Replacement Training Center at Fort McClellan, Alabama, where he was assigned to one of the two all-black infantry training regiments in the U.S. Army. He later credited this experience in preparing him for the changes that would come in race relations in the postwar world.

After VE Day, Winter's destination was to be the Philippines to join an infantry division to prepare for the expected November invasion of Japan. However, the war ended with the dropping of the atomic bombs that summer. His destination remained the same, but the mission changed to one of restoring to civilian status the Filipino guerilla units that had fought the Japanese and to find the enemy soldiers who had taken refuge in the hills after the end of the war.

While in the Philippines, he took part in mopping-up operations over several months and observed the terrible effects of the devastating combat years on the people and the environment of the islands. Seeing the Bataan Death March area and other similar scenes of carnage, Winter experienced the feelings of many who barely missed the fighting. "Scars of the battle were still evident along the roadway," he writes in his memoir. "A flat helmet of the prewar army but then still being worn by the men on Bataan lay in a labyrinth of jungle vines where it had been lost by its nameless owner. As I picked it up, I wondered who he was and what his fate had been. Again I reflected on the vagaries of war that would call on some men to die in the most hopeless and desperate circumstances while sparing others of us to survive."

Winter was part of the military escort from the 86th Division which met General MacArthur at Nichols Field in Manila for the ceremonies granting the Philippines independence on July 4, 1946. Six weeks later Captain Winter returned to California and the civilian world that he had left over three years earlier.

In the fall of 1946 with the support of the GI Bill, Winter enrolled in the University of Mississippi School of Law. He decided to study law because of his father's association of law with the legislative process. Winter says that his father was a "frustrated lawyer" who had always wanted to be an attorney and admired the legal system. This influence and Winter's early fondness for the legislature led him to pursue a law degree. He graduated with the June class of 1949 after serving as the editor of the *Mississippi Law Journal* during the 1948–49 year. He won the Phi Delta Phi award as the Outstanding Law Graduate.

While a freshman in the Law School, Winter and several of his military veteran classmates decided to run for the Mississippi legislature. He challenged a four-term incumbent.

Winter campaigned hard. He revisited all of his old schoolmates, compared war adventures with fellow veterans, reestablished connections with the cotton farmers he had gotten to know in the summer of 1941, met with his father's long-time supporters, and attempted to shake the hand of every qualified voter in the county. He described the campaign as "an exhilarating experience." The result of his first political campaign was election to the Mississippi House of Representatives by a majority of more than three to one. Of the twelve Ole Miss students who made legislative races, eleven were elected. With his swearing-in in 1948, Winter began twenty-five years of public service in state government which included five different elected positions over the period 1948 to 1984.

In 1950 Winter married Elise Varner of Senatobia, the daughter of the long-time mayor of that north Mississippi city. Also in that same year, Winter was asked by U.S. Senator John Stennis to join his staff in Washington, D.C. After the legislative session, he accepted a position as a legislative assistant to succeed Frank Smith who was a candidate for Congress.

In 1951 after running unopposed for reelection to the legislature, he was ordered as a reserve infantry officer to report to the Eighth Infantry Division at Fort Jackson, South Carolina, due to the growing intensity of the Korean War. While serving as an infantry replacement training officer, he was discharged by the Army in December due to the sudden incapacitating illness of his father. He returned to the Mississippi Legislature.

The Washington D.C. position with Senator Stennis had been possible because the Mississippi legislature was part-time duty. There were biennial sessions of usually three months' duration. Regardless of the brevity of the duty, it was Winter's passion. The 1948 legislature in which he and his law classmates were seated was over 50 percent WWII veterans. In their naivete they expected changes to occur due to the changes the war had brought in many aspects of life. Instead they found entrenched opposition to any threat of change to the old order. In his memoir, Winter describes what he and his idealistic fellow freshmen found:

> The leadership was still largely dominated by the most reaction-
> ary and conservative defenders of the economic and social status
> quo. We would soon encounter the political schizophrenia that
> would envelop the Deep South for the next two decades: the com-
> mitment of progressive young Southerners intent on carrying out

their war-born mission of improving the quality of life in their
own communities, and the almost paranoid resistance to any
change that had its focus on race. Many of us believed . . . that
these were not necessarily collision courses and that in empha-
sizing plans for economic development and education we would
achieve the ultimate solutions to our dilemma. Soon we would
find that it would be more complex than that.

Despite their initial disappointment, the young legislators were
determined to push for changes in several areas: workmen's
compensation—Mississippi was the only state that still required
court approval before an injured worker could be compensated—a
four-year medical school, and a relaxation of certain "blue laws"
which prohibited various activities on Sundays. Among Winter's
accomplishments during his three terms in the legislature were
the coauthoring of the Workmen's Compensation Act, working
for the establishment of a four-year University Medical School
in Jackson, and chairing the House Agriculture Committee during his second term.

He also demonstrated his lack of concern about taking
stands on controversial issues by introducing a successful bill
that legalized Sunday afternoon movies. This act was one of the
most bitterly opposed actions of Winter's long career. Another
controversial matter in which Winter was an integral player
involved a leadership issue in the House.

With his uncontested reelection to the legislature for a third
term in 1955, Winter decided to campaign for the Speaker of
the House position—considered the most powerful political
position in the state. The three-term Speaker Walter Sillers of
Rosedale had served in the House since 1916 and had no inten-
tion of stepping down. In his memoir Winter describes Speaker
Sillers: "He was supported by a cast of tough and loyal followers
who also knew the legislative ropes. Personable and gregarious,
Sillers nevertheless ran a tight ship. He was also an unyielding

disciple of what soon came to be known as 'massive resistance.' He was in the words of the day, a 'Delta Bourbon.' He was a force to be reckoned with and certainly not to be confronted."

During their first two terms, Winter's young upstart colleagues had grown frustrated with the lack of progress on issues such as support for public education. Discussions were held concerning a challenge to Sillers. Despite the intense efforts of Winter and his forty loyal supporters, the efforts to unseat the powerful Speaker failed. Although there were consequences for the unsuccessful challengers—Winter lost the chairmanship of the Agriculture Committee—a message had been sent that there was a significant force in the House that advocated change. Several of these challengers to the status quo became lifelong friends and allies of Winter's.

During the 1950s Winter became involved in another of his lifelong passions. Through his father's love of reading history, Winter had developed a love for it at an early age—especially the history of Mississippi. In 1952 he helped to reactivate the long dormant Mississippi Historical Society. In 1954 he became its president. Since then he has been active in all of its activities. He has served on the board of trustees of the State Board of Archives and History continuously since 1957, and as its president since 1973. In 2003 he was honored for his long, diligent work in the field of preserving the record of Mississippi's past when the newly constructed state Archives and History Building was named for him.

In the final days of the 1956 session, Winter learned of the death of the state tax collector. Among the duties of that office was collecting the black market tax on the sale of illegal liquor (see "On Black Market Tax," page 187). Governor Coleman asked Winter to resign his seat in the legislature and appointed him to this office. Winter served the remainder of this term in one of the most interesting and unusual state government positions anywhere in the nation.

Winter who as a legislator had voted for local option on the question of liquor sales was convinced that the tax collector office should be eliminated and the duties given to the state tax commission. The office was a lucrative one. It did not have a salary. Instead the tax collector was paid a commission on the taxes collected. These generous commissions led to Winter's belief that the office could easily generate corruption, and he advocated its abolition. The legislature refused to fold the office into the tax commission so three years after his appointment, he ran for election.

The campaign was a tough one due mainly to his opponents' charges against him of violating the state's prohibition law. Winter's arrangement of an agreement with the state of Louisiana to limit the sale of tax exempt liquor to certified Mississippi wholesalers appeared that he was trying to increase sales of the illegal liquor which had the legal taxes on it. Winter successfully fought an indictment attempt in circuit court by explaining to the grand jury how the system worked. He argued that the more he aggressively collected the tax, the more money would go into the state coffers to fund hospitals and schools.

He faced nine opponents. During this race, Winter was labeled a Coleman man meaning that he was not supportive of gubernatorial candidate and avowed staunch segregationist, Ross Barnett. He was also criticized for not being a member of the White Citizens Council. Winter had declined to join that organization when he was a candidate for the state legislature.

Winter kept his position as state tax collector by winning his first statewide race in 1959. Over the next four years, he continued his advocacy of abolishing the office, and in 1962 the legislature voted to combine the duties of the office with the state tax commission.

In 1963 Winter was elected state treasurer where in addition to overseeing the state's finances, he found opportunities to speak out in "more forceful terms" on the issue of race. During his term as treasurer, Winter had the opportunity to go to New York City as a representative of the state to market bonds which had been issued for various education projects. He used this occasion to try to portray a more moderate view than the one perceived of all Mississippi politicians by the New York financial community. His efforts at changing some of the perceptions were successful, and during his time as state treasurer, he was able to create some strong allies for the state in the national financial circles.

As the election year of 1967 approached, Winter began looking seriously at a race for governor. He felt that the racial unrest of the early sixties was calming somewhat. Paul Johnson, Jr., the governor for the last four years, had served with a quiet dignity that had a moderating affect on the race issue. However, the recognized front runner was again the White Citizens Council's choice. Ross Barnett had served as governor from 1959–1963, and being ineligible to succeed himself, he had sat out for a term. Now he was ready for a second term and was considered the front runner. A possible candidate to oppose him was the lieutenant governor, Carroll Gartin. Gartin was a close personal friend and ally of Winter's. They had commissioned a joint poll to assess their chances when Gartin died unexpectedly.

With his friend's death, Winter decided to run for governor regardless of the poll results. There were many across the state looking for a candidate who could defeat Barnett. However, there was pessimism that anyone could be found. The ideal candidate could not appear to waver on supporting segregation. These political king-makers felt that Winter was too outspoken on the race issue and would be labeled a liberal who would sell out to the demands of the blacks.

Despite advice against running, Winter announced his candidacy with an emphasis on better education and better jobs. Congressman John Bell Williams who had supported the

Republican Barry Goldwater for President and thus had his seniority stripped by his fellow Democrats, decided to come home and run. He became the candidate the anti-Barnett crowd was seeking. Much to Winter's chagrin, Williams was regarded as a moderate alternative to Barnett.

Bill Waller, the prosecutor of the accused murderer of Medgar Evers, and Jimmy Swan, a Hattiesburg radio station owner, joined Winter, Barnett, and Williams in the race. Winter campaigned vigorously, and despite occasional jeers of being a "nigger lover," he gained strong support from the business community and from young voters who were weary of the race-baiting of past campaigns. With Barnett, Williams, and Swan attracting voters from the same pool, Winter led after the first primary.

The runoff was with John Bell Williams. Winter had a very slim lead over Williams after the first vote but was unable to maintain it in the final vote. Despite all of his efforts in a campaign that was physically, emotionally, and financially draining, he suffered his first political defeat.

In 1968 Winter's former employer and political ally, Senator John Stennis, offered to submit his name for consideration for a federal judgeship that was vacant. Although it was an attractive offer, Winter declined the appointment.

Another opportunity emerged with an offer to join one of Jackson's most respected law firms—Watkins, Pyle, Edwards, and Ludlam. Winter accepted and settled into the practice of law.

While practicing law over the next four years, he observed the changes occurring in Mississippi politics—the reduction of covert race-baiting that had been common; the increasing numbers of African Americans becoming eligible to vote; eighteen-year-olds being eligible to vote for the first time; and many Mississippians looking for new, more progressive candidates.

In 1971 Winter decided to run for lieutenant governor, an office that would allow the occupant to work outside of state government.

Winter won the race in the first primary over Cliff Finch, a district attorney from Batesville. Winter was determined to be a successful lieutenant governor—a post that he felt comfortable in after having been in the legislature.

His goals as lieutenant governor continued to be support of public education at a time when massive school desegregation was causing much distraction in many areas. He revised many of the procedures of the state senate and opened government meetings to public scrutiny. All public agency meetings during this time were closed to the press and to the general citizenry. There were several senate changes instigated during his tenure to make the senate run more effectively such as reducing the number of standing committees. In addition, with his endorsement, guidance, and insistence, an open meetings act became law. Winter received an award from the Louisiana-Mississippi Associated Press Association for the passage of this law which opened all public meetings to the general public.

As the election year of 1975 approached, Winter emerged as the clear front-runner for governor. Cliff Finch, Winter's little-known opponent in the lieutenant governor's race, appeared to be the only certain candidate. A district attorney and former supporter of Winter's, Maurice Dantin, decided to enter the race.

Finch ran a populist campaign with the intent to identify with the "working man." The racial issues of past campaigns were not in the forefront. Blacks and whites were attracted to the Finch strategy of working in a different blue collar job each day. In the first primary, Winter led, but Finch was a surprisingly close runner-up. The run-off was three weeks later, and in his memoir Winter writes of those difficult days:

I appeared in the parking area outside of a Jackson industrial plant at six o'clock the next morning. The friendly banter of the earlier campaign was gone. The eyes of many of the workers were hard.

Some refused to take my card. "We're for the working man," they told me. I would hear that many times in the ensuing weeks. . . . Class had now, for this campaign at least, replaced race as the emotional factor. It was "us" against "them," and I was "them." The reaction at the factory gates became increasingly hostile. Some workers refused to shake my hand. Others wondered why I couldn't drive a bulldozer.

Winter lost the 1975 race to Cliff Finch by the largest number of votes in a run-off election in Mississippi's history. Winter decided his quest for governor was a lost cause. He felt that he would never have another chance, therefore he committed to a life outside of politics. Winter remained an interested observer of politics, but returned to the law firm as managing partner.

As the 1979 campaign for governor was well underway, he heard from a former campaign aide who had added Winter's name to a poll that he stood a good chance of being elected. With the discredited Finch administration in some disarray, the voters were favorable to a Winter candidacy. On the day before the qualifying deadline, he entered the race for another try at the governor's office.

This campaign was far different from the previous ones. Winter said, "What we were experiencing was the unpredictable process whereby a political campaign creates a momentum of its own. It was the easiest campaign that I ever made. Everything was falling into place. After two exhausting and brutal races in which I had sustained heartbreaking defeats, I now was enjoying a surge of support that I had not known before."

Winter defeated Lieutenant Governor Evelyn Gandy in the second primary and then defeated Republican nominee, Gil Carmichael, with 61 percent of the vote. On his third attempt he was elected governor of Mississippi.

Winter came to the governorship well prepared. His legislative experience in the House and in the Senate as the presiding

Governor-elect Winter with his wife, Elise Varner Winter, outside their
house in Jackson, November 1979.

officer was especially helpful given the structure of Mississippi's
state government. Under the 1890 Constitution, little authority is vested in the governor and the legislature sets all appro-
priations. Winter's experience with the budget process and the
legislative rules and procedures was invaluable. He also had
a personal acquaintance with many of the lawmakers, several of whom he had known since he first entered the House
in 1948.

Along with this experience, he brought an absolute love
for the job. He thrived in the position. It was evident from the

Governor Winter and First Lady Elise Winter in the Governor's Mansion with their daughters LeLe (standing), Anne (seated in chair), and Eleanor (seated on floor), 1980.

beginning of his administration that he was determined to bring some positive changes to state government.

As governor, Winter's initial priority was to restore integrity to the office. Although he had emphasized education in his prior campaigns, he had not made it a major issue in the 1979 campaign. However, it quickly became a top priority, and he began to explore ways to finance some of his plans for education despite finding a fiscal crisis due primarily to tax cuts initiated during the previous administration.

During his term, legislation was passed to preserve several of the state's natural areas; to improve the open records and meetings laws; to preserve and protect the state's historical structures; to increase the number of women and minorities appointed to boards and commissions; and to professionalize many of the positions in state government, i.e., the director of the Board of Economic Development had been a political appointee.

Education became the center of his and his staff's efforts. As his attempts to improve education in Mississippi increased, national attention became focused on this issue. A campaign was launched by his staff to influence the public to pressure the legislators to address Winter's plan for massive changes in the antiquated system. The final result was achieved with much national acclaim.

The Education Reform Act of 1982 was the crowning achievement of his administration. Henceforth, Winter was known as the "Education Governor." Several fellow southern governors followed his example in crafting similar education legislation in their states—Bill Clinton in Arkansas, Dick Riley in South Carolina, and Lamar Alexander in Tennessee. With the passage of this legislation to restructure K-12 education, Mississippi became the leader of the education reform movement that swept the nation in the late 1980s and early 1990s.

During his four years as governor, Winter was active in regional and national organizations. He served as chairman of the Southern Regional Education Board and the Southern Growth Policies Board. He was active in the National Governors Association where he was often asked for advice on education reform.

As his successful four years approached an end in January of 1984, the chancellorship at the University of Mississippi began to be mentioned as a possibility with the retirement of the current chancellor announced for later that year. A majority of the tenured faculty at the University formally endorsed the appointment of Winter. The Board of Trustees of the Institutions of Higher Learning offered the job to Winter. Winter accepted and then three days later he announced a change of plans.

With assurances of support from various national democratic party groups, Winter announced in the early spring of 1984 that he would challenge U.S. Senator Thad Cochran. He realized the race would be a difficult one to win due to Cochran's popularity and because the election was occurring during the reelection campaign of the overwhelmingly popular Republican president, Ronald Reagan. The last campaign of his long political career—one that included ten races, seven statewide—was unsuccessful.

With this final political venture behind him, Winter was set to return to his law firm. However, before he could resume his practice, he was accepted as a "Fellow" at the Institute of Politics which was sponsored by the John F. Kennedy School of Government at Harvard University. This opportunity of meeting and discussing various national issues with other policymakers from around the nation during the spring semester of 1985 was an exciting experience for him.

In the fall of 1985 he returned to the law firm. In addition to the practice of law, he became involved in many of his interests in both the private and public sectors. Free from the restraints of political life, Winter entered a stage of his life that he refers to as "enjoyable and free to pursue whatever course desired." During this twenty-year period he has remained very active in education, racial reconciliation, community service, open and responsible government, preservation of historical records, economic development, and church activities.

His involvement in education has been and continues to be at all levels including constant advocacy for a statewide four-year-olds program in the public schools. In 1989 he held the Eudora Welty Professorship of Southern Studies at Millsaps College where he lectured primarily on southern politics. At the University of Mississippi Law School he was the Jamie Whitten Professor of Law and Government where in the fall of 1989 he lectured on law and public policy. Also at Ole Miss a distinguished chair in history is currently endowed in his honor. For four years he was

Distinguished Professor at Mississippi Valley State University. He has received several honorary doctorates from distinguished institutions of higher learning around the South.

The William Winter Teacher Scholar Loan Program is a state-funded recruiting program for K-12 teachers named in his honor. In 2001 Winter received the Martin Luther King, Jr., Memorial Award in Education from the National Education Association. During the 2005 legislative session, he co-chaired the Coalition for Children and Public Education which was active in efforts to assure adequate funding for the public schools.

In the other area of his most intense interest—racial reconciliation—he served on President Clinton's Advisory Board on Race. An offspring of his involvement on this board is the William Winter Institute for Racial Reconciliation at the University of Mississippi.

Winter has served as chairman of the Kettering Foundation which gives grants to community development projects around the nation. He is a founder of the Foundation for the Mid South which is devoted to the educational and economic development of Mississippi, Louisiana, and Arkansas. He has served as chairman of the National Civic League and as chairman of the National Commission on State and Local Public Service.

In 2005 the Mississippi Forestry Association honored Winter as the State Tree Farmer of the Year for his conservation efforts on the same family farm in Grenada County where he was reared.

At the time of this publication, William and Elise Winter live in Jackson, Mississippi. They have three daughters and five grandchildren. He remains at age eighty-three extremely active in all the various areas he has contributed to over his long career. He continues to have a full schedule and is a speaker in much demand around the state and nation.

—ANDREW P. MULLINS, JR.

THE MEASURE OF OUR DAYS

Oh Lord, we thank thee for the opportunity of living in this good land in these days of change and challenge. Will thou give us the courage and the vision to use this time to make our country a better place; where respect for the past will not be regarded as blind reaction and where the hope of the future will not lie in destroying all that has gone before; where integrity will be placed before advantage and the search for truth will be our ultimate effort; where compassion shall always temper our triumphs and honor shall attend our defeats; where the most privileged of our citizenry shall live without dominating and the most deprived shall live without fear of domination; and where all of us may have the grace and understanding that come from knowing thee. Amen.

—WILLIAM WINTER
National Prayer Breakfast, Washington D.C., 1983.

GOVERNMENT

Governor William Winter and President-elect Bill Clinton, Renaissance Weekend, Hilton Head Island, South Carolina, December 1992. President Clinton would later appoint Winter to the President's Commission on Race.

ON DEMOCRACY

The processes of democracy will work only as they reflect a degree of self-restraint on the part of the citizenry. This was the dream that Jefferson had—that in spite of the skeptics, human beings were indeed capable of governing themselves. This has been a noble experiment, but the experiment has not yet been concluded. It is still up to us to prove that there are enough people who will temper their own desires and demands with a concern for the public good.

I am not certain that after almost two centuries this revolutionary concept of self-government can or will be sustained. I am distressed by the evidence of so much public irresponsibility abroad in the land. I am concerned that so many political decisions are influenced by selfish special-interest groups with no apparent concern for the welfare of others.

But the fact that we do have these abuses still does not discredit the system. What they do point up is . . . that more than ever our political system just must have the participation of more . . . who have the good sense and the dedication to see to it that the right attitudes prevail.

We do this not by singling out for our opposition some unfortunate official who may have voted against a specific proposal in which we were interested, regardless of how he may have voted the rest of the time. Too frequently are we parties to denying public office to able and conscientious men simply

because out of their conscientiousness they not always have
seen things our way.

—"The Retail Merchant and His State Government," speech, Convention of Mississippi Retail
Merchants Association, Biloxi, Mississippi, July 25, 1966.

More of our citizens must be involved in the decision-making
that affects their lives . . . communities do not exist just for the
economically fortunate or the socially privileged.

—Remarks, 99th National Conference on Governance.

Our political system is a reflection of our collective values
and priorities. So first of all there must be a change in those
priorities . . . there must be more of a willingness on the part
of all of us to respond to leaders who will challenge us to make
hard decisions. Those of us who have seriously worked at it
for any length of time know that making democracy function
properly has never been easy. It is when we try to make it too
easy that we get into trouble. It is more than slogans and shibboleths and flag-waving.

—Speech, University of Texas LBJ School of Government, May 23, 1992.

ON LIBERAL VS. CONSERVATIVE

There are few words in the English language that are more
recklessly used or generally misunderstood than those two
verbal packages of political dynamite, "liberal" and "conservative." They have, in fact, acquired so many distorted
definitions as to make them almost meaningless. Actually
most of us have a philosophy that combines some of both
words. In its true sense "liberal" means generous, open, and
compassionate, reflecting a willingness to accept new ideas
and better ways of doing things. Most of us want to be like
that, and in that sense we are liberal. On the other hand,
"conservative" means stable, traditional, and respectful of

established values. And most of us want to be like that, too. There really should be no contradiction in all this. One set of values is needed to support the other. I suppose we would all agree that the most basic and conservative of our ideals lies in our respect for human life and the dignity and integrity of the individual. But to protect those conservative values we must rely on the application of the liberal concepts of free speech, worship, and assembly as provided in the Bill of Rights. This is the paradox—the most certain and stable guarantee of our own basic rights lies in the extension of that guaranty to those with whom we disagree. We must use liberal values if we are to preserve conservative institutions.

—Television commentary, WJTV, Jackson, Mississippi, 1985.

ON BUREAUCRACY

From time to time during the past forty years, as occasion seemed to demand, there has been tacked on a commission here and a bureau there . . . we have different departments, commissions, and other agencies functioning as official state bodies . . . almost every one of which is separate and independent from all the others. . . . We have outgrown our administrative organization, and the efforts to modernize it have resulted in a complex, confusing, costly, inefficient system, noted for its decentralization of authority and diffusions of responsibility. Functions overlap, jurisdictions conflict, services are duplicated, and waste and confusion result, all resulting in increased burdens upon the taxpaying public.

—Speech, Common Cause, Jackson, Mississippi, January 13, 1979.

Nowhere is the expression, "Don't rock the boat," more appropriately applied than to public administration. Having a low profile is usually considered as more desirable than being a boat rocker. Whistle-blowers get into trouble. Paper shufflers don't. The bureaucracy protects its own. In my experience in state government, I have found most individual employees genuinely wanting to do a good job. Some saw ways to do a better job, but they often felt frustrated by the inertia that opposes change.

—Television commentary, WJTV, Jackson, Mississippi, 1985.

There is no more determined defender of territory than the embattled guardian of the political status quo.

—Speech, University of Texas LBJ School of Government, May 23, 1992.

ON LEGISLATORS

It is especially in legislative activity that the problem of accommodation by way of compromise comes up most frequently. Administrators have their problems, but they do not so often involve differences of opinion within the framework of government itself.

. . . I cannot recall a single instance in which any piece of legislation that might be termed controversial was ever passed without some modification in the nature of compromise. Many of these changes were agreed to in a sincere belief that they would in fact strengthen the legislation. In other cases they were acquiesced in merely because they seemed necessary to pass the bill.

. . . It has been my good fortune during my career to have been rather closely associated with many legislators . . . not only from my state but from . . . many other states. These were men and women of diverse social, economic, and political backgrounds—of varied levels of education and with differing concepts of government. But it has been a basis of much encouragement to me to note the sense of responsibility to the public interest that has been reflected in the expressions and actions of the vast majority of those officials. . . . And in those instances that we might cite where they may have been less than responsible, it all too often has been because a less than understanding public has by indifference or delusion encouraged them to act irresponsibly.

To one who has not experienced them, it is hard to picture accurately the pressures to which a legislator is subjected, but I can tell you from experience that it is frequently a lonely feeling that one has as he contemplates taking a position which conviction dictates when seemingly all of the advocates are on the other side. It is the ability of highly organized special interest groups frequently to direct these pressures that poses a continuing threat to the democratic process. This is where the public official must be supported by an alert, intelligent, informed citizenry, conscious of its duty to be responsible, too. For after all responsibility mirrors responsibility.

—"In Defense of the Practical Politician," speech, Centre College, Danville, Kentucky, April 1962.

There was for instance the day the dog bill came up. It was to raise revenue by imposing a head tax of a dollar a dog on every unfortunate canine in the state. Debate was heated between the pro-dog and the anti-dog forces. Then in a major compromise effort the ultimate amendment was offered—to permit the exemption of one bitch and one son of a bitch in each household. Someone asked the respected Oscar Johnston what he thought about it. "Can't vote for it," he said. "Might exempt the head of the family."

—Unpublished personal memoirs.

ON GOVERNMENT

We hear much about what the government should do for the individual. We hear very little about what the individual should do for his government—the part he can play in the formation of public opinion.

If the governments are sometimes autocratic or tyrannical, it must be primarily because there is no constituency behind them with a sufficient respect for the duties and obligations of a courageous citizenship. How did it happen, for instance, that such a well-educated people as the Germans allowed Nazism to flourish? Was Christianity dormant?

There must be something else developed within the individual in resistance to the human failings that have caused us at times to sell ourselves for a few pieces of silver or to ignore the twitchings of an ever-present conscience.

Whatever approach we take, therefore, we come back to the individual and the task the individual must perform in his own life. But it will be said, this has long been clear, and it is man's own indifference or selfishness, or greed, or blindness to folly which bars the way to understanding. We see the consequences—wars between nations, wars between groups within our own country, friction in the courts, friction on the industrial front, and friction in the home. We know that human friction needs a solvent. Without spiritual help, however, there can be little diminution of that friction.

One of our difficulties today is that we are always advocating "permanent" solutions of present-day problems. Many of them are unsolvable today. They may be solved when the rule of reason is applied. Solutions sometimes come when both sides in a dispute recognize that there is no solution in sight. The moment we decide what is or is not solvable in life, we make real progress toward an ultimate solution. For as we devise ways and means of living with insolubility, we apply the rule of reason to solutions we never conceived of before.

. . . Impatience is the forerunner of anger. Patience is the most essential ingredient of human love.

—Speech, Rotary Club, 1960s.

You have been asking with a great deal of concern, "What has happened to states rights?" You are saying that we have heard a lot of loud talking about states rights, but all the while we have seen the voice of the states steadily decrease. We have had plenty of lip service given to the concept of states rights, but we have had precious little action designed to preserve them. And some of those who have done the most talking about states rights have done the most to tear them down.

We have got to understand that the only way that we can give any sort of meaning to this process is by making certain that we have a state leadership that will add strength and dignity to state government and that will see to it that government at the state level is responsive to the needs of the people. No matter how much the words "states rights" are spoken, it does not help the cause of states rights if the state leadership cannot command respect.

To make the voice of Mississippi speak effectively in the councils of the nation we just have to have the leadership that understands what to say and how to say it—and sometimes more importantly what not to say and when not to say it . . . loud words and flailing arms are no substitute for common sense and self-restraint in the building of good state government. And lashing out with irresponsible attacks on everything and everybody outside the state doesn't put any meat on the table inside the state.

What we need to help build up the principle of states rights is a leadership that will concern itself with finding ways for the state to meet its obligations to its people on its own initiative instead of forever reacting negatively to ideas proposed from outside. . . . States rights will be successfully defended not by using up all our energy fighting outside enemies but by using more of our energy in promoting inside programs.

—Speech, Wayne County Fair, Mississippi, September 22, 1966.

As the complexities of living increase and as the task of providing public services for an urbanized society becomes more difficult, the demands of the public do not diminish but instead seem to increase. Even though the problems are vastly more complicated and involved than they were in a simpler and less urgent age, many people still expect, even to a greater degree than ever, that simple, quick and direct solutions be provided for most of their dilemmas.

. . . We who wear the cloak of public office have a special duty under these pressures to make certain that we do not compound the problem by presuming to have all of the solutions neatly packaged and tied with a little pink ribbon. The task that we have . . . is more clearly to try to delineate what is within the reasonable and legitimate province of political or governmental action and what is outside the scope of our ability and our authority.

This is not easy, and it may not be popular. But I am convinced that sooner or later we are going to have to do a better job of establishing the boundaries of legitimate and proper concern for ourselves as guardians of the public interest.

Too many citizens in this country have been sold on the idea that for every problem that confronts them not only is there a quick and decisive solution but that there is a quick and decisive political solution. If this is a logical premise, then the rest of the premise is that we simply find the politician who says he has the solution, and all of our troubles will be over. . . . This premise is not reliable, and we are confronted with many problems today for which the answer lies only in slow, patient, and time-consuming remedies, many of them outside the ability of government to provide at all.

I think that a great deal of the disillusionment about public officials and the processes of government is based on this false assumption that all of the woes of humanity can be solved by political action and the appropriation of money. . . . I sense a growing danger that out of this disillusionment the political fabric of this country can be torn apart by the charlatans of both the left and the right who prey on the very discontent and disillusionment that they have helped to create.

I think that it is a legitimate concern of ours then that as the guardians of the gates of government at the basic grassroots level we make certain that we help create attitudes in our respective communities that will put proper limits on what the public will look to us to do. This means that government at the municipal level ought to concentrate on establishing some urgent and reasonable priorities that it will insist on meeting adequately come what may, and not spread itself thinly and inadequately over too wide a range of activities.

For example, there are some obvious priorities that have to be met if you are to have a good city. Without drawing any hard and fast lines, I would say that law enforcement and public education would be the two areas of public service that a progressive city must establish as the most basic of all needs. There are obviously many other vital services . . . that have to be provided, and I do not minimize them. The point is that any community that feels that it can cut corners by skimping on its law-enforcement system or on its educational system, in which I specifically include its library, is asking for trouble.

The maintenance of law and order and the existence of an educated citizenry just have to come before anything else, and they have to be provided even if it means leaving off more popular but less essential services somewhere else. . . . I emphasize this in order that we may try to avoid the pitfalls of seeming to have a ready answer for everything that comes up.

I have seen this tendency as a member of the legislature where so frequently individuals and groups come at the slightest excuse for legislative relief for problems that should be solved in the private sector. It is my point of view that we should not use political action to try to come to grips with so many everyday difficulties of modern life. Certainly we should not until we have applied remedies outside the scope of governmental involvement. This is getting harder and harder to do—to resist this temptation of letting an impersonal force come up with what appear to be the easy answers. But we have to work at it.

As our society becomes more and more an urban society, it is going to take greater and greater effort to preserve the values that helped make this country the greatest nation in the world. It is much harder in this highly urbanized system that is the result of more people living closer together to maintain the real meaning of the values of self-reliance and initiative and independence.

The very nature of urban living almost insists that we blend in and conform. There is in fact a tendency on the part of some of us in public life to be a little impatient with the individualist who insists on being an individual. It is frequently much more comfortable for us to deal with people in the mass where a pattern of behavior can be predicted. But a part of our responsibility lies in helping encourage more people to preserve as much as they can of their independence and their individuality. For only in this way do we keep the basis of independent judgment that this country must have.

There is a danger that too many of our people will succumb to the fatal resignation of just being one of the crowd. And when enough of them lose their will to act as individuals, we shall have slipped into the twilight of our country's greatness. When we get to this point where the poll-takers and the image-makers can tell us in advance what we like for breakfast and what kind of mouthwash we shall use and whom we shall elect to public office, we really are in trouble.

. . . We talk about the great society, but a free society can be a great society only as enough of us assume the moral responsibility to meet the obligations of freedom. . . . Serving responsibly in positions of public trust has never been an easy task, and today it is rendered even more difficult. But because it is difficult means that it is more important than ever that we give our best.

—Speech, Urban Affairs Conference, University of Mississippi, October 21, 1966.

I believe that government ought to be carried on so that people have an opportunity to know and understand what is going on, and to that end, I believe that more of our public affairs ought to be carried on in open meetings under the full scrutiny of anyone who wants to see how his business is being carried on. This has been one of the things that Watergate has emphasized to the American people, and I want to see our government in Mississippi carried on with as much openness as possible.

—Speech, Neshoba County Fair, Philadelphia, Mississippi, 1974.

There is no subject which can create more confusion and mis-understanding than the financing of government.

—Television commentary, WJTV, Jackson, Mississippi, 1985.

When I came to the governor's office in Mississippi in 1980, I found my fellow governors in the midst of an intense debate over a concept called the "New Federalism."

. . . The so-called New Federalism has to involve more than a shuffling-off to the states the ever-increasing costs of providing essential services. What also must be understood is the wide difference in fiscal capacity existing among the different states. The concept of federalism will not work unless it leads to a removing of barriers that effectively prevent people in one area from sharing in the basic opportunities enjoyed by people in the rest of the country—barriers that are frequently represented by state lines.

. . . There is a national stake in this. As a country, we cannot continue to be compartmentalized into the haves and have-nots by the accident of geographic boundaries. In the development of human resources, in the quality of health care, and in the enjoyment of the opportunity to make an adequate living, there must be a source of national commitment that transcends states and regions. As a nation we are now competing on a global basis. If as a result of diminished resources, the people living in one particular state are unable to develop competitively, the national capacity to compete is reduced proportionately.

This is what a renewed concept of federalism must be about. We must find a way to use our total national resources to reduce the inequities arising from the historic fiscal disparity among the states. The answer obviously does not lie in imposing substantial new financial burdens on have-not states now struggling to meet existing responsibilities. This brings us to three fundamental national objectives. . . . First, there must be a general agreement on what constitutes a basic minimum level of essential public services. Second, each state should have the capacity out of its own resources or through a sharing of national resources to maintain that agreed on basic level of services. Third, the location and funding of national projects should be based at least in part on the consideration of achieving a parity of opportunity among all states.

Attaining these objectives is now made more difficult by a new development—the greatly diminished capacity of the federal government to allocate resources to attain this kind of balance. The simple truth is that the central government, weakened by . . . years of unprecedented budget deficits, can no longer be relied on for creative leadership and responsible initiatives in solving the nation's most difficult domestic problems.

Some have suggested that under these grim new realities, we turn back to the examples of an older time when private charities were looked to as major providers of relief to the poor, sick, and elderly. No one can deny the significant contributions to our national well-being made by the generous spirit of private philanthropy. It is to be hoped that the tax relief granted at the national level in recent years will prove an additional incentive for substantially increased private sector giving.

By no stretch of the imagination, however, can a largely uncoordinated surge of voluntary contributions be considered an effective response to a society as massive in its needs and diverse in its structure as is America. . . . Compounding the problem further is the unhappy fact that the areas most in need of support are usually the ones most removed from the major sources of private philanthropy.

Much the same thing can be said of the role of public-private partnerships. Without diminishing the place that such arrangements can have in addressing public problems, it seems unrealistic to put too heavy a political and social burden on the business and corporate community. There will be many instances where a public-private partnership can fill a pressing need, but we must remember that private businesses can operate successfully only as long as they are financially viable. Their role in the present dilemma of federalism, therefore, must be looked at as strictly supplementary.

Where then do we turn in our search for answers to this vexing problem? One answer at least lies in the building of stronger and more responsive government at the state and local level. Accustomed for years to being portrayed as hopelessly inept and lacking the creativity or capacity to provide solutions to local problems, these levels of government have now demonstrated that they are more alert to the needs of society than the big brother in Washington. Some of the best administered governments in the country are found in the state houses and city halls, where under the force of necessity resourceful solutions are being crafted for age-old problems.

. . . With limited local resources and reduced federal capacity, there seems little alternative except for states and their political subdivisions to reorganize themselves in ways that will increase their own capacity and efficiency. This can lead to better local government and thus a strengthening of the federal system where it counts the most—in the state capitols, city halls, and county courthouses.

. . . Still, in the final analysis, there must be a leavening process that can only take place through a national effort. The restoration of a fiscally sound national government that has the flexibility and capacity to act is an essential element in maintaining an effective federal system. More than the preservation of a formal political structure depends on it. The fulfillment of the nations' destiny as measured in the maximum productivity and well-being of all its people must remain the over-riding objective.

—"Federalism in a Time of Fiscal Austerity," article written on June 2, 1988.

The only thing that will make a difference in government and in our larger society is the performance of the individual human beings who make up the system. This is why it is so vital that we maintain the concept that public service is a noble and worthy calling.

. . . Our system must constantly look at ways to reform itself. We need more boat-rockers in government—men and women who are willing to use their creative skills in devising better ways to do things.

. . . Both those who work in government and those who are the beneficiaries of that work have a joint responsibility. Public servants must remember that they are just that and that their duty is to the taxpayers who pay their salary . . . private citizens and the organized groups which increasingly speak for them must recognize the limits of what they can reasonably expect from government.

. . . We cannot allow ourselves to fall victim to the skepticism and cynicism that limits our capacity. No nation endowed as richly as this one can ever permit the voices of pessimism to overcome the high purpose that has sustained us so far.

. . . We must rely on a new kind of interdependence that recognizes the indispensable role of government but only as it is based on the communitarian values of a civil society. No democratic government can mandate or enforce those values. It can only reflect them and use them in advancing the cause of freedom and justice. The base of this strength will not— must not—be looked for in some charismatic leader or popular cause. It can only be found in the most durable institutions of our society—in the home and in the family, in the great educational institutions . . . where the qualities of tolerance and compassion and truth are espoused and defended, and it will be found ultimately in the temples of the human spirit.

Because we have been so favored . . . we have much that is required of us. In spite of the mistakes and missed opportunities of the past, in spite of the abuse of our human and natural resources, in spite of the elements that at times have separated us from each other, our nation and its political system remain reservoirs of incredible vitality and strength.

—Speech, University of Texas LBJ School of Government, May 23, 1992.

At every level of government there are obvious outmoded barriers to good performance. . . . They are usually hard to remove. For what we are talking about is turf-protection, and there is no more determined resister to change than the politician or bureaucrat whose job may seem threatened or whose way of doing things may be affected.

. . . The process of governing in our country is a two-way street. It demands responsible citizens as well as responsible politicians. Government cannot mandate the values by which we live. It can only reflect those values that the people feel are valid. . . . The political values on which all of us must rely need to be tried and tested in the hard crucible of experience.

They cannot be subject to giddy and frivolous whims based on images created in thirty-second sound bites.

—Speech, National Association of Secretaries of State, Portland, Maine, August 11, 1992.

In an age when the public becomes more and more impatient for visible results and tends to think of public affairs in thirty-second sound bites on the six o'clock television news, the pressure on political leadership frequently causes it to seek initiatives that promise immediate benefits regardless of how they may affect long-term strategic planning.

As a former governor I know firsthand about these pressures. For more than a century . . . Mississippi has been confronted with a massive array of social and economic problems going all the way back to the Civil War.

. . . The difficulty has been not so much a failure of political leadership to recognize the needs as it has been an inability to approach on a long-range basis the means whereby the problems could be addressed.

More and more states are coming around to a recognition of the importance of strategic planning for the long term. . . . There also seems to be a growing recognition of the complex relationships that now exist between national and international policies and state strategies. There is an increasing awareness that failure to anticipate and take into account future trends can present intractable problems.

This makes for a certain paradox, for now the forces of change move with such swiftness that they quickly render out of date many state initiatives even before they can be fully implemented. No longer do we have the luxury of leisurely adjustment. This new dynamism makes all the more urgent the establishment of a process for strategic planning that can adjust for unexpected change. Flexibility and adaptability are now the key elements in keeping state government on the right track.

All of this has to be understood in the context of two very fundamental considerations. The first is a recognition of the increased complexity of public issues and the fact that in most instances there are no quick and easy solutions. The second is the imperative that the public understand what is going on and to the extent practicable be involved in what is going on. Both of these factors put an added responsibility on those who govern to keep the public informed. This informing process has to be believable, though. It cannot be a mere public relations gimmick. . . . Citizens will rally to the support of causes which require commitment and sacrifice if they perceive them to be of worth to their children and grandchildren even if they themselves may not be directly benefitted.

To tap into this kind of commitment requires of public officials a renouncing of the cynical manipulation of public opinion that has so often reduced the noble field of politics to a cold and calculating game. It means a lessened dependence on the kind of synthetic media hype that tends to make into a simplistic formula the solutions to complex problems.

It has been these unfortunate developments in the communications process between public officials and their constituents that have increased this skepticism toward government.

—"Governing for the Long Term," writings completed on November 30, 1994.

The more front-line public employees are encouraged to share in the rationale behind policy decisions and are permitted to participate in planning the means of implementing those decisions on a day-to-day basis, the better they perform and the better the system works.

. . . Significant public policy is not always made behind the closed doors in the state capitol or in the courthouses. Public policy can be made out on the streets and in community groups. It's the most effective public policy of all because it bears the imprimatur of the people themselves and their representatives take heed of those appeals.

. . . Only when we create a political atmosphere where there is a genuine opportunity for people to feel that their participation and their views are going to contribute to a desired result do we establish credibility for meaningful reform, for meaningful public policy. It's harder to make public decisions that way. It would be a lot easier for a small number of us . . . to make those decisions for everybody.

. . . There's a lot of cynicism in the body politic these days. The way to remove it is to engage more people in the task of public problem solving. If we do not build from the bottom up we will suffer from the top down. Devolution, if properly responded to by dedicated citizen action, can represent a huge gain in advancing the well-being of our society. Left to flounder in citizen apathy and distrust, it can be a betrayal of our better nature.

—"Reflections on Public Participation in Our Democracy," speech, Devolution Initiative Networking Meeting, Jackson, Mississippi, January 26, 1999.

POLITICS AND LEADERSHIP

The "Boys of Spring" gather at the Governor's Mansion on December 20, 1982, to celebrate the successful passage of the Education Reform Act of 1982. From left— Andy Mullins, Dick Molpus, David Crews, Bill Gartin, John Henegan, Governor Winter, and Ray Mabus.

ON THE ART OF COMPROMISE

Men who have made great contributions . . . by their ability to bring issues to workable solutions . . . these were not grim, narrow-minded fanatics insistent on every letter of their position as if it were providentially inspired. These rather were reasonable men, conscious that they did not have all the answers and willing to concede to others the possibility that they, too, might be at least partially right. For it can be only on this basis that compromise can be entertained.

So in this somewhat less than perfect world in which we find ourselves living let us get a few things straight about what we are talking about. . . . There are indeed few absolutes. So much of what we hold to in politics or economics or even in religion is conditioned to a large extent by the circumstances and experiences of our individual lives.

In a society as diverse as the American society of today, it is manifestly out of the question for our government to operate except on the basis of a recognition of different and even diametrically opposing viewpoints and of a willingness to accommodate those differences. There is nothing new about this either, for there exists no more historic example of compromise intelligently arrived at and honorably carried out than that afforded in the Constitutional Convention of 1787. This is the spirit of compromise as it was demonstrated in its most exalted hour.

. . . They were practical men at Philadelphia in 1787, as indeed they had to be, who could understand that the realization of their noblest hopes and dreams lay only through the processes of earnest conciliation and agreement.

. . . It is one thing to look at this process from the standpoint of issues, though, and quite another to look at it from the standpoint of individuals. This is where more real anguish is involved for sincere and honest men than in any other area of political experience. What legislator worth his salt has not lain awake at night and wrestled with his conscience as he pondered the eternal problem of expedience versus judgment. Compromise is very definitely represented here, and again it should not automatically be made a matter of reproach. It is not merely cynical to say that a defeated politician can't help anybody. It is an ever-present fact of life that an incumbent ignores at his peril.

But whether we approach the subject from the point of view of issues or individuals, it seems that we come quickly and inevitably to this conclusion: That compromise per se is not only not bad but on the other hand is as necessary as breathing. The problem is not if but when and possibly how. The legitimate use of this complex art must therefore be our concern, rather than whether we should practice it. Subject to admitted variations as to times, places, circumstances, and methods, there stands out this general rule that seems to afford a minimum standard to follow in making this judgment of what is proper: Will the public interest ultimately be served by a process that will be consistent with the self-respect, morality, and integrity of the individuals responsible for the decision?

. . . The efficacy of the application of such a rule will of course depend on the sincerity, intelligence, and honesty of the individuals, but then must not all legitimate compromise rest on the same basis? . . . Any kind of compromise that has to be enforced with a loaded pistol is of course not really compromise at all.

There is one other quality that I have not mentioned that is largely overlooked in thinking of compromise, and that is the element of courage. The general tendency is to assume that any politician who ever concedes anything is lacking in courage. Frequently, the very opposite is true. In many cases, perhaps in most, the willingness to compromise involves great courage, and the more sharply defined the issues and the more deeply divided the partisans, the greater the courage that is required. Some of the most courageous public officials I know have been the quietly dedicated men of reason who have worked under the most unrelenting pressures to gain acceptance of unpopular but necessary agreements, while bombastic orators denounced them as traitors or worse.

. . . It is in its application rather than its definition, there-fore, that we can understand what compromise means. It is here that we must go if we shall be able fully to appreciate it as a working process in a free society operating under a demo-cratic political system such as we know in this country. A totalitarian system need not be concerned with compromise as a tool of government. We must be.

It seems to be a fact of history that under the American system of government, the process of compromise has been relatively successful in dealing with procedural differences and lesser substantive issues. But when it has come to the really great questions of civil war and the division of the Union, of slavery in the nineteenth century and its progeny, the racial problems of today, there frequently just has not existed the consensus, the willingness to approach a workable solution short of sharp and open conflict, that these issues demand. That this is true is usually no accident either, for the partisans work overtime to see to it that nothing less than total accep-tance of their view is tolerated.

. . . History does not usually move in straight lines to real-ize predetermined programs of reform, and the absolutists, with no sense of the art of compromise, have all too often been rendered totally ineffectual in causes that frequently had great merit. What so many of these starry-eyed idealists could never bring themselves to understand was that in the world of politics, of all places, there is seldom room for total victory.

. . . It has remained therefore for the practical practitioners of the political arts to temper and to put into effect what in many cases have started out to be the programs of dreamers. . . . And in more cases than not it took horse-trading to do it. There is not cynicism in this. It is merely a recognition of how in our system, legitimate though admittedly less than perfect ends are arrived at.

—"In Defense of the Practical Politician," speech, Centre College, Danville, Kentucky, April 1962.

ON LEADERSHIP

This is a time when the fraternity concept is under attack. This puts upon us a special responsibility to do those things which strengthen that concept. We must justify our existence. Why do we have this organization? Is it to build houses and win trophies and have banquets? These are means. Is it to increase academic achievement? Partially. Is it to elect campus officers? Partially. Is it to have a good time? Partially. Is it to render service to others? Partially. Is it to build friendships? Partially. The high calling of this organization is to do all these things as a means of attaining this final and noble end—of developing distinctly uncommon men capable of rising to heights of leadership in their chosen field.

—Speech given to his fraternity at the University of Mississippi when Winter was eighteen years of age, 1941; found on the back of an envelope in the Winter papers, William F. Winter Archives and History Building.

The great and overriding need of our state and our country is for men who will use their talents and abilities and time in the building up of the society of which they are a part. We have always had our share of those who have been quick to find fault, who have been expert at viewing with alarm, who have been full of pessimism and discouragement. We have many of these people today. These are the people who look out on the world around them with a frustration and discontent born more out of their own inadequacy and limitations than from the shortcomings of the world about them.

We have always had examples of many people in all ages who have thought that the world was going to pot. History does not seem to remember too many of these people for very long, however, for in the implacable course of human events the forces of change and the processes of progress have swept aside those who have not been able to assimilate the challenges and the opportunities of the world around them.

. . . It takes no special genius, it takes no great quality of leadership to tell our fellow man what is wrong, but it does take a superior quality of leadership and a deep insight into history and into people to provide effective answers.

—Speech, Jaycees Banquet, Meridian, Mississippi, January 29, 1966.

The Bible tells us "Where there is no vision, the people perish." This ought to have special meaning to anyone aspiring to public leadership, for under our system, unless we have enough public officials who have enough vision or just plain good judgment and common sense to keep us on the right track, we are not going to be able to make it.

For the problems are not going to get simpler; they are going to get bigger and more complicated, and we are going to have to have more men and women in politics and government with the ability not only to solve these problems, but to head some of them off in advance.

. . . But it is not enough to understand what ought to be done. Effective leadership is involved in knowing how to get things done. This involves being able to get people of diverse backgrounds to work together. We have a state of widely differing interests with people of every conceivable background. We cannot afford to let our differences interfere with our ability to work together effectively.

. . . There must be a leadership based on an openness and willingness to communicate with the people. . . . Leadership has to be based on a testing under fire. I know that the political arena is not an easy or comfortable place to be these days, but I have worked with the people of this state long enough to believe that they will respond to a leadership that will tell it like it is. I . . . have not always been on the popular side of every issue and I have been punished for that politically from time to time. I do believe . . . that we are at a point in the history of our great state where you want to hear the facts without sugar-coating and without being kidded in order that we can fully realize the great potential that is ours.

—Speech, Neshoba County Fair, Philadelphia, Mississippi, 1974.

Management is really what the governor's office is all about—management of money, of programs, but most importantly, of people. A governor succeeds or fails almost in direct proportion to the caliber of the people that he surrounds himself with.

—Television commentary, WJTV, Jackson, Mississippi, 1985.

It is difficult to lead further than we have gone ourselves. Many of our former leaders—in business and in politics—never aspired to looking beyond their own narrow and familiar borders. Intimidated by new and different ideas, they sought refuge in the comfortable and the familiar.

. . . What is important? It frequently depends on one's point of view or personal interest. This is the most pressing demand of citizen leadership, whether in business, government, or the professions. It is to enable more of our fellow citizens to look beyond themselves, to cut through the irrelevant and understand where their real interests lie.

. . . How little public officials can accomplish unless they are sustained and supported by committed and enlightened citizen leaders with no special axes to grind.

. . . Change through political action does not come easily or automatically. It comes only as enough interest is generated by those who have the capacity to lead. But the capacity to lead is not enough. The actual molding and creating of public opinion requires aggressive action if significant change is to occur.

. . . The approach and solutions to . . . problems cannot be left to chance decisions by the indifferent and the uninformed. They cannot be run away from. They cannot be ignored. This is where the role of the citizen leader is absolutely essential.

. . . It is the transforming leader who makes the difference, who does not ask the question, "What's in it for me." It is this type leader who confronts the problems of his community and seeks to address the needs. There are not enough willing to make that sacrifice, because it comes at the expense sometimes of lost business and lost friends—still it is only through this process that progress is made.

. . . Where is much of this new leadership coming from? One of the most obvious and heretofore underutilized sources will be from the ranks of women. One significant reason for this is that we are moving now from management to leadership. Leadership that focuses on bringing out the best responses in others, that inspires, that enables people to adapt quickly to change. Women will be the new leaders because they are now coming into their own in the business and professional establishment. They have now reached a critical mass in virtually all the white collar professions.

. . . This new leadership must also come and will come increasingly from those elements of our diverse citizenry who for too long have been excluded—from blacks and from recent

immigrants who are now winning their spurs as able and visionary men and women capable of meeting any challenge.
—Speech, Leadership Florida, Orlando, Florida, March 24, 1990.

The truth is that the development of leadership is a never-ending process. . . . The task of all of us remains, as it has been since the founding of this republic, to put our best efforts and our best qualities into the governance of our country and its various subdivisions. Our democratic system does not permit the luxury of withdrawal. When the problems loom the most difficult and dangerous, the greater is our responsibility to be in the arena.

. . . Where does leadership begin? It begins with good citizenship. No one can rightfully claim the mantel of leadership who has not demonstrated the qualities of good citizenship.
—Speech, University of Montevallo, April 11, 1991.

. . . Our responsibility to improve society and to face the tough issues that confront us does not end at the board meeting. The true leaders . . . are those who lead by their personal example. . . . It often takes enormous personal courage to work for a true and just society if it means going against what is the popular social norm of our own comfortable, middle class environment.
—Speech, Philanthropist Day Luncheon, Jackson, Mississippi, November 17, 1992.

. . . What we are really talking about is elevating to a higher degree of importance that one quality that ought to set public officials apart and that should be the defining qualification for public office. That . . . is the capacity for leadership and all that that abused and overused word implies.

. . . A political leader can effectively serve the public interest only as he or she is able to inspire and encourage a sufficient number of citizens to join in a social contract for the improvement of society. That really should be the only justification for public service. It is the only kind of public service that can make a difference and that will bring about the achievement of a truly good and just society.

. . . The transforming leader . . . is concerned with leading his constituents to goals beyond their own vision and experience. This type leadership is more interested in the promotion of the more permanent values of justice and equity. Frequently these purposes are harder to articulate or explain than more mundane and tangible needs as represented by lakes and dams. This is not to say that the latter are not important. It is simply to emphasize that the long view will almost always involve the raising of the sights of people who too often have their eyes on immediate objectives that they can see and comprehend.

This . . . is the most vital challenge facing state political leaders. . . . There must be a willingness on the part of more officials to put the long-term public interest ahead of personal political safety. I know that this is sound public policy. It may also be good politics. At a time when there is the growing disillusionment with politics and politicians, it may be that the best way to restore the essential element of trust in our system is for the political leaders to move to the top of their agenda proposals to address the long-range problems that gnaw at our economic and social stability.

—"Governing for the Long Term," writings completed on November 30, 1994.

What now are the legitimate priorities of leadership? First and foremost must be a commitment to the maximum development of our people. The formation of human capital is where we must concentrate our energies. Undeveloped human capital is our greatest barrier to growth and prosperity.

A second priority must be the eliminating of the fault lines that still divide us, whether those divisions be based on race or class or religion or geographic location or anything else. We must understand that the building of a spirit of community is an indispensable element of leadership.

. . . We must confront doubt and cynicism with a true
vision of a better life that can be achieved only through the creation of a civil society that is based on fairness and justice, on
equity in the market place and on recognition that we live in a
social contract with each other.

—"Visions for Leadership," speech, leadership seminar sponsored by University of Southern
Mississippi, Gulfport, Mississippi, October 3, 1996.

One does not deliberately charge windmills, but there come
times when you have to be willing to lay your career on the line
on issues that cannot be compromised.

. . . When one is elected to lead, there comes the sobering
realization that the long struggle to lead is empty and unsatis-
factory unless it is accompanied by a commitment to achieve
established and worthy goals.

. . . Essential to effective leadership . . . is the quality of persistence. There are few quick and easy victories on issues that
really matter and about which people hold strong opinions.
Victory seldom comes to the fainthearted or the short-winded.
And there are few permanent and lasting victories. The causes
for which we fight have to be sustained by continuing effort
over long periods of time.

. . . But for all of us there are the setbacks that test our commitment and challenge our purpose. This is the ultimate test
of leadership—to maintain one's own ability to see a desired
result achieved and to transmit that commitment to others.

Most of all we must not be afraid to fail. We must be willing to take chances and defy risks, stretching ourselves at times
to limits that may exceed our grasp but that in the stretching
will add to our strength and resiliency.

. . . There is another area of our national life that calls for
responsible citizen leadership. It has somehow become fash-
ionable if not downright patriotic to regard our political process as unworthy of our participation and government as our

enemy. . . . Without condoning the various errors and weaknesses that we can attribute to our politicians and our political system . . . that system is the basis of our freedoms and liberties, of the stability of our civil and economic institutions, of our capacity to provide for the education, the safety, the security and general well-being of all of us and to protect the weak from the raw power of the strong.

In the well-meaning (and perhaps not so well-meaning) efforts of some to denigrate the political system by calling up its failures to the exclusion of its glorious triumphs, we diminish the one element that is essential to the preservation of our country, and that is the continuing faith of its people in the integrity and efficacy of that system. This is where strong leadership is needed—to stand resolutely against those in politics who get elected by denouncing as unworthy the very government which they propose to serve.

—"Leadership and Ethics," speech, Kellogg Foundation, New Orleans, Louisiana, February 22, 2000.

ON POLITICIANS

It is the lot sooner or later of almost every person who has devoted his full efforts to elective political office to lose a race. There is no reward in politics for second place. Close does not count. It only makes more painful the sting of defeat. It is one of the harsh and brutal realities of the most demanding and exacting of human activities.

—Unpublished personal memoirs.

The most effective political executives and legislators have been by and large the men who have come out of politically oriented backgrounds. One of the greatest problems that that essentially reasonable man, Dwight D. Eisenhower, had to adjust to as president was the infinitely more difficult role of executing and administering policies in a civilian atmosphere than in the arbitrary military world to which he was accustomed.

. . . In every crisis and in the formulation of every great decision to meet that crisis, it has been the decent practical politician, with his sense of proportion, who more often than not has pulled us through.

. . . So, when all is said and done, we owe much to the practical politician and the adjustments that he brings to the inexact science of government. If he is less than certain, it is because he knows . . . that certitude is not always the test of certainty. If he is less than an intellectual, it is because he knows that all the answers are not found in books. If he is less than perfect, it is because he is dealing with less than perfect men. For in this sometimes lied-about, much talked-about, and almost universally misunderstood character of the political stage lies the highest hope for the fulfillment of the American dream but more than that the faith and the determination that the cause of freedom will endure.

—"In Defense of the Practical Politician," speech, Centre College, Danville, Kentucky, April 1962.

The one essential ingredient of a successful politician is his or her ability to communicate with the public. In a world where the sheer volume of messages being sent out makes it difficult for us to hear anything above the din, the ability to attract and hold listeners for any length of time is almost impossible. People also would rather hear the good news than the bad. That's how so many of the old-style politicians got elected—by holding out to folks, many of whom were having an awful hard time, the expectation that things were going to get better. People vote for hope, and they also vote for a simplification of complex problems. They don't like to read the fine print. But the way the message is delivered is the key. That is frequently

more important than the message itself. It, of course, helps if
the message is also important.

—Television commentary, WJTV, Jackson, Mississippi, 1985.

There is no more defensive person in the world than a politician whose turf is threatened.

—Speech, National Civic League, Charlotte, North Carolina, November 12, 1988.

The political roadsides are littered with the bones of dead politicians who ignored one fundamental fact: They did not live up
to the expectations of the people who elected them. In many
cases that has been because in seeking office the politicians
had promised results that exceeded their capacity to produce.
In other instances it has been the consequence of a misunderstanding about the time frame in which political action could
achieve results.

It is the latter circumstance that poses the greater hazard
to the conscientious politician as well as to the body politic.
A candidate may over-promise at his or her peril. Pie in the
sky has always been a staple commodity in American politics.
There is even a cynical assumption by some voters that campaign pledges automatically become void after the election.

—"Governing for the Long Term," writings completed on November 30, 1994.

Ex-governors have a hard time. I didn't realize how tough it
was until I was down in Pascagoula, Mississippi, not too long
ago. I came out of the courthouse, and saw a man looking at me
very intently. Finally this man blurted out, "Ain't you William
Winter?" Now I didn't know whether that was a friendly question or not, but I admitted that I was who he thought I was.
He said, "I thought you were dead." I said, "I'm just politically
dead." That seemed to make him feel better.

—"Reflections on Public Participation in Our Democracy," speech, Devolution Initiative
Networking Meeting, Jackson, Mississippi, January 26, 1999.

ON POLITICIANS AND JOURNALISTS

Politicians and journalists have traveled a long and tortuous road together. Since the beginning of the republic they have borne the responsibility of creating a citizen awareness of the process of governing that is indispensable under our political system. But it has not been a straight road that they have traveled nor one that has ever been fully understood by either. Always natural adversaries, dominated by strong personalities and victimized by vanity and conceit on both sides, politicians and the press have combined to focus attention on the best and worst of both worlds.

. . . Running through much of the political and journalistic rhetoric in our state and raising it to a more intense pitch was usually the element of race. It is difficult to conclude where the initiative was—whether it was a press responding to a public opinion inflamed by political demagoguery or whether it was the voice of the press itself which was primarily responsible for creating such public opinion in the first place. It was probably a little of both.

. . . With only a few exceptions the press and politicians alike fell victims to a siege-like mentality that dulled their senses to many of the really pressing issues like quality education, transportation, healthcare, and our relations with the rest of the country. In too many instances the press's sole criterion for judging a politician's performance was his record on the maintenance of the status quo. It was almost impossible under the intimidating presence of the White Citizens Council, which was publishing its own newspaper, to have issues considered except under the measuring stick of race.

. . . The decade from the late fifties through the sixties was not a happy period for Mississippi journalists or politicians. To some extent they had become prisoners of a state of mind that they had both combined to create, and they found themselves on a racial roller coaster that was difficult to control. No moderately inclined politician could stick his head up without running the risk of journalistic decapitation at the hand of some of the vilest poison pen-wielders ever to write a commentary. It was . . . simply matter-of-fact character assassination that did not rely on anything but raw racial prejudice. It permeated the coverage of political races from governor to supervisor and invaded practically every story involving governmental affairs.

. . . In some of the great issue battles of the last fifty years the leadership of the press was more often than not a critical factor. It might even be said in a number of those instances that its support created the winning side. Perhaps the most dramatic example of this was in the passage of the 1982 Education Reform Act. There is no question that the support of the press . . . provided the ultimate momentum that enabled that significant legislation to be passed. That was almost a classic example of the press working in a way that mobilized public opinion to overcome great legislative resistance.

. . . So as we understand that politicians and journalists are natural adversaries, we must also know that their roles, their perspectives, and their priorities are different. Neither can be perceived by a skeptical public as being obligated to or dominated by the other. At the same time, though, they share two indispensable obligations. The first and most important is simply to help make workable and manageable a public policy process that will serve the maximum good of all. The second is the dependence that each has on the other for the establishing and disseminating of reliable and accurate information on public issues.

. . . The last twenty years has produced both in this state and on a national basis a series of dramatic changes in the relationship between the press and the politicians. The issues, or at least public interest in the issues, were not exactly the same for Mississippi as for the nation. For the nation in the middle and late sixties, it was the Vietnam War and civil rights. In Mississippi it was resistance to the civil rights movement. In both instances, however, an increasingly skeptical press began asking tougher questions of political leaders.

. . . It must be acknowledged that as long as there is human frailty and vanity there will always be an uneven relationship between politicians and the press.

. . . It is to hope that [responsible journalism] will result in a citizenry that is more informed and therefore more responsible. That, after all, is what a free press is all about. That is what the First Amendment is all about. And that is what politics is supposed to be all about. For all of the excesses on both sides, and there have been many, there remains the basic foundation on which our free society rests, and that is the ultimate good sense and sound judgment of the individual citizen who makes up the body politic.

—Article, *Journal of Mississippi History*, 1986.

ON POLITICS AND THE POLITICAL SYSTEM

Just one week ago I returned from six days in the Soviet Union, or at least what is left of the Soviet Union. While the Union itself may be struggling to create a new political identity, there has already been created among millions of Russian people a sense of what it is to achieve personal freedom. From them I learned in the short space of those few days as much about my own country as I did about theirs.

. . . What I saw and heard in those days portrayed for me more graphically than any experience that I have ever had what freedom of speech and worship and assembly mean to a people who have never known them. I cannot predict what is ultimately going to happen in Russia. Their economic problems

are so great as to defy comprehension. Many of the people are
still numb from the effects of a system that did not permit
them to have any control over their lives. The grocery shelves
are bare, and for many physical survival is the first concern.
Snow already covered the ground, and the winds straight off the
Arctic tundra gave credence to the prediction of an unusually
harsh winter. It is for them, in the words of Thomas Paine, "a
time that tries men's souls." . . . We Americans, of all people,
ought to understand what this is about.

And what it is about is the endless struggle to create and
the even harder struggle to sustain a political system that
ensures the greatest good for the greatest number and that does
it in a way that protects the individual rights and liberties of
the least among that number. This is no inconsiderable task,
as the Russians are finding, and that we ought to know but too
frequently forget.

The paradox that we are confronted with today is that the
Russians seem more concerned with protecting their recently
achieved democratic system than we do in supporting a tried
and proven one. . . . The public polls indicate that fewer and
fewer people in this country believe that government matters
anymore. Cynicism and apathy threaten to overwhelm our
system.

. . . What is going on is that we have been through a period
when we have seen ambitious politicians get elected by pro-
claiming our system corrupt and the government our enemy.
And then as if fulfilling that description, we have watched our
schools decline, our cities deteriorate, and crime, poverty, and
economic problems increase. No wonder a prominent national
politician was moved to lament, "The voters are angry and
alienated. They believe we stand for nothing." What we also
know, though, is that despite the frustrations with contempo-
rary politics, most people have not turned their backs on
civic duty.

. . . What we are really talking about is the maintenance of a civil society that is based on the ideals of citizenship under law: in freedom of speech, of the press, of assembly, and of worship; and in the protection of minority rights under majority rule. This all starts in the guarantees of the First Amendment, without which the later guarantees of the Fourteenth would hold scant meaning.

They form the basis for the sustaining of a healthy body politic. If we do not use these principles for the reinvigorating of our political processes, we shall see a further erosion of the vitality necessary to maintain a just and orderly society.

When alienation from the system becomes too great, there is a tendency for people to lash out in disturbing ways. This lashing out, if it becomes extreme enough, can pose a serious threat to our political institutions and our personal liberties. As these frustrations grow, we begin to look around for someone to blame. Many times that anger will be directed toward those who are different from us or who hold fundamentally different views. And the more complicated and pervasive the problems that confront us, the greater is our tendency to look for simplistic answers. . . . Weary of hearing messages that we do not understand or simply do not want to hear, we wind up shooting the messenger.

What we must not overlook is that we live in an increasingly pluralistic society. As a consequence, there can never be the kind of social or political or religious conformity that many who yearn for a simpler time would like to establish.

. . . We have, of course, been through times like these before. In the face of our real or imagined fears, we have been temporarily beguiled by those who promised us security from the troubling problems swirling around us.

. . . The danger remains . . . that in our zeal for quick and simple answers we shall continue to ignore both the lessons of history and the mandates of the First Amendment. There is always with us in a legal system like ours the dynamic tension between the rights of the individual citizen and the maintenance of a stable social order. It is a process that must be able to distinguish between superficial and temporary concerns on the one hand and a clear and present danger on the other. It is one thing to burn a flag on the Capitol steps. It is quite another to burn the Capitol. We must continue to remind ourselves of the difference.

What is really at stake here is our ability to build a society that is capable of minimizing our cultural and ethnic and religious differences as we elevate to the highest priority the dignity of the individual. But that process is not without its difficulties. A free society obviously does not imply a total absence of restraint. It is in maintaining this narrow and sensitive balance that we must all be involved.

. . . In the face of all of the tensions and frustrations and fears to which we are all subjected today, our task must be to make certain that we are not caught up in the passions and emotions that would substitute temporary comfort and convenience for the tried and tested verities that have marked our constitutional journey. Given our own long and eventful history, we should be reassured by the success thus far of our common effort. And with that recognition and assurance, we should be inspired to pursue that journey into the future unafraid.

—"Some Reflections on Politics and the First Amendment," speech, Mississippi Jefferson Meeting, Mississippi College, Clinton, Mississippi, November 9, 1991.

In a world riven by religious and ethnic and class division, the United States of America doesn't need to fall victim to this kind of divisiveness that this campaign [presidential election of 1992] is in danger of creating. Our historic strength has been over the capacity to build on our diversity and to broaden the circle of humanity who found peace and refuge in this good land.

That has been the historic strength of our two-party system—that no matter how we differed on the issues of the day we did not make our campaigns a kind of holy war. We did not create some mythical code of values which we required our fellow citizens to embrace lest they somehow be regarded as less than true Americans.

. . . Those of us who have served in elective office know or we certainly ought to know that our capacity to govern effectively is in almost direct proportion to our ability to bring people of different viewpoints together in a way that produces beneficial results. The most effective political leaders that I have known have been those who have been able to see more than one side to an issue and who have been able to accommodate diverse views in achieving desirable objectives.

—Editorial, August 26, 1992.

The task for us who are or who have been involved actively in politics is to restore the confidence of the people in the political process. And without that confidence there is no way the system is going to work.

. . . What is behind much of the present disenchantment with politics is partially the result of the increased impact of political decisions on our lives coupled with the increased complexity of the process by which these decisions are made. Added to that is a more extensive media coverage of those decisions but a media coverage that does not necessarily provide the kind of relevant and understandable information that citizens are looking for. The result is a lot of confusion about what is really going on.

As the political stakes become higher and the individual feels less and less relevant, we are seeing at the same time the emergence of highly organized, well-financed special interest groups. Accompanying this depersonalization of politics is the appalling increase in the amount of money that is now involved in political campaigns. The average citizen is beginning to believe that he or she has been shunted aside and the organized special interests have taken over.

. . . Is it possible that one of our problems now is that we have embraced a new and different kind of naivete? In a much more complex environment we look for unrealistically simplistic solutions for political problems that have no easy answers. We have come to feel that some program or process is going to make things better. In our frustration we keep looking for that silver bullet that will solve all our difficulties. We try to find the answer in term limitations and balanced budget amendments and all manner of regulatory restraints, the usual effect of which is to hamper the effective performance of honest and dedicated public servants.

. . . Is it not naive to accept the proposition that we can expect to receive ever expanding services and entitlements from government without having to pay for them? This may be the most difficult trend of all to deal with. This is one of the most frustrating connections to make . . . between the conscientious public official and a public that has become increasingly concerned with what it can get from the system. Citizens must understand that they cannot have it both ways. They cannot demand responsible performance from their government unless they are willing to be responsible in what they require of their government.

The exclusive or even primary pursuit of self-interest is almost a sure-fire way to create a system that will ultimately break down. . . . Too many citizens have been encouraged to adopt a policy of getting while the getting was good. For some that meant taking advantage of the perquisites of public office. But for too many of us ordinary citizens it has meant claiming all the benefits that the system could make available whether we paid for them or not.

Is it not naive to make one narrow issue the ultimate test in our political decision-making? . . . Our broad and diverse society cannot be governed properly unless we can put the interests of the larger community ahead of our special and even selfish concerns. It is in the formation and operation of so many well-financed and organized lobbying groups that there develops a disconnection between the people and their officials. Somehow the disproportionate influence of these groups must be diminished.

We must understand that our political system is a reflection of our collective values and priorities. It is here that we must make the corrections if we are going to fix the system.

. . . Making democracy function better has never been easy. It is when we try to make it too easy that we get into trouble.

. . . It will be a continuing, never-ending process of self-analysis of what is wrong and of how we can improve it. There are no quick fixes.

. . . Our system must constantly look at ways to reform itself. We need more . . . men and women of creative insight who can use their skills and their intellect to devise better ways to do things. Rewarding resourceful and innovative leaders and holding them up for the public to see is a good way to reduce cynicism and discontent about how the system works.

. . . The one thing that has most turned off and alienated the American people from their political leaders . . . has been the impression that they are afraid to make tough decisions and that they are driven by public opinion polls. . . . I believe that more can be done to restore confidence in our system by political leaders being willing to go out on a limb in support of positions that may not necessarily be popular but which can be defended as serving the public interest.

. . . The worst mistake that any of us can make is to assume that the people are turned off by politics. They are turned off by politics and politicians that they believe to be self-serving and unconcerned about them.

. . . For the ultimate success of our system is based on the confidence of the people in its integrity and its commitment to the advancement of the communal values of a civil society.

—Speech, National Association of Secretaries of State, Portland, Maine, August 11, 1992.

To hear some people tell it, the state of politics in our country today is worse than it used to be. Acknowledging that it has a lot wrong with it, I am convinced that on balance the state of our political system is more acceptable than was the case when I entered politics over a half-century ago. The biggest thing wrong with it now is the inordinate amount of money it takes to run for office. Those huge campaign contributions have a certain corrupting effect.

The biggest thing wrong then was that our political system back then excluded so many people. When I was first elected to the legislature, there were no black voters in my county, even though half the people in the county were black. We gave almost no thought to the effect of public policies on the environment. We did not think it necessary to educate more than a small fraction of our people. We had little concern for the conditions under which thousands of people worked.

We spent more time passing laws to keep people from going to the movies on Sunday afternoon or drinking a glass of wine than we did on providing adequate schools for everybody.

Here are some of the questions that we ought to be asking now about our political system. Is it sensitive to the needs of the people as a whole and not just those who make the largest campaign contributions? Is it dedicated to bringing people of different racial and ethnic and religious backgrounds together? Is it a process that accentuates our common humanity and advances the ideal that we are indeed our brother's and sister's keeper?

—Speech, Grace Chapel Presbyterian Church, Madison, Mississippi, July 30, 2000.

In politics, there frequently develops a perceptible momentum that seems to defy the sources of conventional wisdom. It can be felt but not always measured, even by sophisticated polling.

. . . Campaigns are costly in terms of human emotion and physical exertion. . . . It is an axiom of political life that campaign debts for winners are relatively easy to reduce. For losers it is another story. . . . It is a price that understandably has kept many aspiring candidates out of politics. It is a price that unfortunately continues to escalate. It is the largest single threat to our system of free and open elections.

Political campaigns in some respects are like wars. One day you are totally involved in an unforgiving battle to survive, and the next day all the guns are silent. The unceasing activity of pursuing the voters stops dead away. The crowds have gone home. The cheering as well as the heckling has stopped. You are back doing what individuals normally do and wondering in your quieter, saner moments what mad influence drove you to do what you had just been through.

—Unpublished personal memoirs.

JUSTICE AND THE LAW

John C. Stennis and Lieutenant Governor William Winter, Fulton Chapel, University of Mississippi, 1975. Before running for the U.S. Senate in 1947, John Stennis served five years as a prosecuting attorney and ten years as a circuit judge.

ON JUDGES

Among my earliest remembrances of the positive influences and experiences which attracted me to the legal profession were those associated with some of those judges who as a schoolboy I had the opportunity to observe as they came to my hometown of Grenada to hold terms of court. They were in my youthful imagining men of wisdom and vision and possessing power beyond my comprehending. Even though in those days they wore no robes and the courtroom in which they held forth was plain and unimpressive, they appeared to me as towering figures exemplifying my loftiest ideals of what our system of government and jurisprudence was all about. And that is still how judges ought to be regarded, not just by small boys but by all of us.

These particular judges were undoubtedly to be admired but they were also men of their own time, even as we all are, subject to being moved and shaped by their own life experiences and the product for better or worse of the circumstances of their birth and upbringing. Some could be rightly said to be learned in the law; others were less so. Some were technicians fascinated with the intricacies of process in the administering of the law. Some were broad generalists more concerned with simply arriving at the fairest possible result under a given set of facts. But all by virtue of their position were deserving of respect and were accorded that respect by the people whom they served. Some of them were truly notable and were destined for roles of historic leadership in the future.

. . . To a greater extent than any other of our democratic structures, the members of the judiciary are dependent on the faith and confidence of the people for the enforcement of their judgments. They . . . have the power to cite for contempt and to issue appropriate orders for the implementing of their decrees. But what they are dependent on in the final analysis is the willingness of the citizens to respect and obey their decisions. When that respect and obedience are lacking, the system breaks down.

. . . In spite of all of the deep divisions over slavery, trade, and the federal system itself a united country has been able to emerge. That has been largely because of judicial leadership, unfettered by narrow constitutional limitations, that has been wise and strong enough to override the political passions of the moment. Only when the courts have been overwhelmed by those passions, as they were by the traumatic events of the 1850s, has there been a failure to resolve great issues through the civil process.

This is not to diminish the seriousness of the many challenges that have tested the judiciary over the years. . . . The courts have been at the center of some of the country's gravest and most controversial issues. But only because of their political independence have the judges been able to bring some degree of certainty and finality to the handling of knotty problems that elected politicians were just not able to deal with.

The fact of the matter, like it or not, is that as former Chief Justice Charles Evans Hughes said, "The Constitution is what the judges say it is." In the more earthy baseball language of the colorful and fabled umpire Bill Klem, "It ain't nothing till I call it."

. . . All of this is simply to underscore how vitally important it is that we recognize the judiciary at all levels for what it is, and that is the force on which ultimately the stability of our entire political system depends. That is why all of us and most particularly we lawyers must insist on having only those representing the very highest caliber of our profession to be tapped for service on the bench.

And that is why we must never let ourselves in this state fall victim to a system of judicial selection that is dominated by narrow partisan interests whether from the left or from the right. Candidates for judicial positions should never have to seek election on the basis of declaring in advance how they would rule in a given case, and they should not be obliged to raise inordinate amounts of campaign funds in order to seek judicial office. No judge can perform with an essential degree of self-respect and the respect of the public if he or she is unable to exercise judgment free of political pressure.

. . . Judges as individuals and the judiciary as an institution, by virtue of their inherited status as the ultimate guarantors of our commitment to equity and justice and to the maintenance of a stable and orderly society, have an inescapable obligation to exemplify that commitment in all that they do. This obligation extends beyond the formal performance on the bench. Whether you think it should be that way or not, the very nature of their role in society requires judges to be above the coarse and careless conduct that marks and mars the lives of many of our fellow citizens.

Most importantly in a society that seems increasingly skeptical and even cynical about our most revered and established institutions, I believe that the judges have a duty to reenforce the faith of the people in those institutions—in our system of government, in the family, in the schools that educate our children, in the different communities of faith that permeate our culture, in the increasing array of philanthropic entities from the business, labor, and nonprofit world, and in the countless organizations of a civil society that set our nation apart from all others. This should not be done as a blind defense of those institutions and their admitted deficiencies but as a challenge to them to live up to the noble purposes which are their reason for being.

The judiciary must be the force that raises our sights and diminishes our fears and prejudices. The judges must be the guardians of our most basic values and also the advocates of our highest ideals. They in short should regard themselves as a moral force, not in a narrow puritanical sense but as indisputable proponents of a social order that respects the dignity and integrity of every human being. It should be the aim of every judge to try to contribute to a process that will cause all who enter the halls of a courthouse in whatever capacity—as litigant, counsel, witness, juror, or observer—to emerge with an enhanced respect for our system of jurisprudence.

That will mean in many instances an expedited process of arriving at a just result. It will mean developing more efficient ways to resolve disputes and to simplify issues. It will mean retaining a sense of humility and a sense of honor and a sense of balance. It will in short always require the display of those qualities that every good judge should have—wisdom, vision, integrity, civility, and common sense.

And in the future those are qualities that we shall need more than ever to see us through the antagonisms and divisions that can threaten our unity as a people. This country is rapidly becoming the most racially and ethnically diverse democracy in the world. . . . Legal issues revolving around differences of race, religion, and cultural mores continue to create widespread tensions despite all of the progress that we have made in eliminating so much that was blatantly discriminatory in our society.

. . . It is obviously too big a burden to continue to impose on the courts the solution of all of those problems. But again no persons are better positioned to help bring reasonable and civil points of view to these issues than are the judges—both in their official judicial role and in their even more vital role as community leaders and centers of civic influence.

Judges and lawyers must understand better than anybody else that there are usually two or more sides to almost every public issue. In a society as diverse as ours each of us must work at the task of understanding and reconciling the point of view of others with different life experiences from our own.

. . . Our diverse society needs all the help it can get from its wisest and most sensitive and perceptive members to keep it functioning smoothly. I suggest that we turn once more to our own profession and particularly to those who are commissioned to make wise decisions—our judges—to keep things calm and rational. At times in the past we have not always made the wisest decisions on issues where feelings ran high, and we paid a bitter price.

John Dewey said, "Judges not only live in their own generation but they participate in the vision of the future." That it seems to me states the ultimate challenge and the ultimate responsibility. Providing the leadership to create a vision of the future that will diminish the elements that divide us and that will multiply the forces that unify us is a task from which none of us who have taken the oath as members of the Bar can escape.

Judge Irving Goldberg, as a member of the Court of Appeals for the Fifth Circuit, said that judges not only have the opportunity but the duty to speak always for the highest moral values of our society, and when they do not do that, they diminish their authority.

It is this role of moral and ethical leadership that the members of the judiciary and the Bar must continue to fill if our state and nation are to overcome the remaining barriers of economic inequity and social neglect. While a virtuous society cannot be mandated, a base and uncaring society can certainly be discouraged.

—"Honoring the Judges," The Judge William C. Keady Distinguished Lecture Series V, Hinds County Bar Association Meeting, Jackson, Mississippi, May 4, 2000.

ON LAWYERS AND THE
LEGAL PROFESSION

The nature of the lawyer's training, his background, his professional duties require him to be interested in government—indeed to be a part of government. Every lawyer who enters a courtroom, by virtue of his profession, automatically becomes a public official—an officer of the Court, charged with the duty of helping to preserve the efficiency and the integrity of the judicial branch of our government. I do not minimize this role, for certainly the ability of the judicial branch to perform its function depends in large measure on the attitude and conduct of the Bar.

. . . I would hope to suggest an interest and participation in government far beyond this highly limited connotation. For the legal profession in our society is far too broad, far too influential, far too vital to relegate governmental activities, outside the demands of the profession itself, to non-lawyers. And more than that, our country, our state, and our community expect and have a right to expect more of us than that.

What then is the proper and legitimate role of the lawyer in government? Is it to attempt to control every facet of political activity by insuring that no one but lawyers shall hold office or shall exercise the powers of office? Does it mean that all of us should . . . qualify at once as a candidate for every office in sight? Is this to imply that unless one has been trained formally in the legal profession, he is rendered valueless to render competent public service? To give an affirmative answer to questions such as those would . . . be to miss the entire point. I am not necessarily talking about participation in politics as that term is usually understood, although there is a great need for more competently trained lawyers to offer for election to governmental posts, particularly to the legislature. What I am talking about and what I am disturbed about is the infinitely greater need for participation on the part of the average practitioner in the great political and governmental decisions of our state and nation—not as a public official but as a lawyer. No other group in our society is so prepared by formal training and by the experience of his profession to contribute to the solution of public problems or to take the lead in the advancement of causes for the common good. The lawyer's power of analysis, his capacity to marshal facts, his ability to persuade make him a servant of inestimable value in this area of difficulty and division. And in the great conflicts and crises of our history it has been the leadership of the lawyers that has seen us through. This call to greatness, answered in earlier years of our history, now once more requires of us a renewed sense of devotion and dedication.

To bring this demand down to specific terms, it means simply that dedication to the interests of our clients is not enough—not enough for us as citizens—not enough for us as lawyers. This is not to suggest that we should not fight for our clients with all of the skill and perseverance at our command. But it means, too, that in serving the interests of our clients, we do not do so at the jeopardy of the public interest. If this country is to survive, it needs the help of lawyers like one that I can think of who is consulted by legislators to aid in the formulation of legislation which may affect adversely clients whom he regularly represents. He is sought not because of his clients but in spite of them. He is sought because he understands that a good lawyer is more than a good lawyer. He is sought because he is a person who places values in their proper perspective.

We are now living in a society that has a greater need for unselfish, patriotic leadership than was the case in the infinitely simpler, less sophisticated era of Jefferson and Madison. . . . And if our government and our people prove unable to cope with the ever-increasing problems of the future, I think it can be safely said it was due to a lack of responsibility on the part of too many of us as to what we expect and demand from government. The most disturbing fact of life about the operation of our legislatures at all levels of government is the tremendous pressure which is placed upon them by a divisive multitude of special interest groups. As one who sat in the state legislature . . . who as an aide to Senator John Stennis has observed the situation on both the state and national scene, I can tell you that we are in danger of becoming a government by pressure groups. I mention this for two reasons: 1. In far too many cases we find too many able, persuasive, and articulate lawyers moving into a role as spokesman for some of those interest groups that operate on a "vote-for-this-or-else" basis. 2. Public-spirited members of the Bar are in a position to render untold service to their country by helping hard-pressed legislators to resist these pressures. In far too many cases, however, we find lawyers welcoming the opportunity to shun this responsibility and slamming their office doors with a parting shot at politics as "dirty business."

When less was at stake, it seems to me more lawyers made interest in government their business or at least a part of their business. And when they did, the prestige of the legal profession was never higher. The people automatically looked to the Bar for leadership, and they had every reason to expect that they would get it. But gradually we have seemed to shy away from so much of that which we used to welcome, and as we have shunned responsibility except insofar as our clients were involved, we have tended to forfeit our leadership. Let us not deceive ourselves in this. We can regain our standing only by reasserting our leadership, even if it may come at the expense of some of our financial security.

In the golden years of the profession's public leadership—in the first fifty years of our nation's history—we see in men like . . . Alexander Hamilton and John Marshall those qualities of independence, of judgment, and pride in the shaping of

political decisions such as were not to be found later on. These
men spoke with the conscious authority of men who build
civilizations.

Of course the passage of time tends to distort perspective and throw strange shadows. All of those early lawyer-
statesmen were by no means totally selfless in their patriotism.
Take Daniel Webster, for instance; Senator Webster, when the
renewal of the charter of the Second Bank of the United States
was before the Senate, wrote his client Nicholas Biddle: "I
believe that my retainer has not been renewed or refreshed as
usual. If it be wished that my relation to the Bank should be
continued, it may be well to send me the usual retainer."

Many observers join in bemoaning the decline of the Bar's
general participation in public affairs. Dos Passos in 1907 noted
a transformation "from a profession to a business." Woodrow
Wilson thought that over-specialization tended to withdraw
lawyers from their traditional contact with public issues.

. . . It is a melancholy fact that in the Mississippi legislature
a lawyer's position of influence is achieved in most cases in
spite of and not because of the fact that he is a lawyer. If you
want to insure certain defeat for a measure, just be sure that it
gets tagged as a "lawyer's bill." In many of the attitudes of the
legislature there is reflected a considerable measure of distrust
of our profession.

This, of course, is regrettable, but it is not without explana-
tion. The only time a member of the legislature, as a legislator,
has any dealing with most lawyers is on those frequent occasions when the lawyer has a proposal which for a fee he is seeking to pass or defeat in the legislature. How many times have
we shown enough concern in a matter before the legislature in
which we or our client had no special interest to go out of our
way to counsel with members of the legislature thereon? We
need to do more than we have done in asserting constructive
and positive influence in matters of public interest.

. . . We underestimate ourselves and our profession as a factor for good. Let us do more lest we lose our capacity for political achievement.

—"The Role of the Lawyer in Government," speech, 1963.

As a lawyer, I like to think that ours is a profession that has a front row seat at more of the fascinating events that mankind is a party to than any other. And more often than not we find ourselves in the arena in some form or fashion—frequently as combatant, sometimes as arbiter, occasionally as victim. But the point is that we are where the action is, and ours is a life-long exercise in the activities of our fellow human beings. If nothing else is said of us worthy of remembrance, it ought to be at least that we live and work in the mainstream of human affairs. And I would hope that we could have said of us that as a profession we had some hand in determining the way that stream flowed. The point that I make simply is that as lawyers, whether we like it or not, whether we want to be or not, we are irrevocably committed, by virtue of the fact that we are lawyers, to a direct participation in the shaping of the kind of society in which we live.

This is a duty which I must say frankly I think too many of us have tried to shrink from. There have been too many of us who have been unwilling to assert the influence that membership in the Bar imposes upon us. Too many of us have tended to underestimate the capacity for constructive direction that we are capable of giving a society that is often frantically looking for guidance and direction. Let us better understand the significant role that we are privileged to play, indeed, that we must play if the institutions to which we give lip service—institutions like freedom and justice and honor—and law—are going to survive as meaningful elements in the conduct of human affairs. These idealistic concepts and the more tangible systems to which they give rise, such as our judiciary, our legislatures, and our processes of political administration, can ultimately be protected only as the members of the Bar concern themselves with upholding these concepts and institutions.

. . . Let me cite what I consider to be the great and overriding challenge to us as a profession. It is a challenge the answer to which I feel can well determine the kind of nation we shall have in the future. I refer to the massive and frightening assaults which are being made in this country of ours on the established precepts of law and justice and good order.

. . . The structure of our political system cannot endure the emergence of a concept of human behavior . . . that is based on the idea that if you don't like a law or a system of law enforcement, you not only don't have to obey the law but you can deliberately defy it.

. . . There cannot be any such thing as "limited lawlessness." When respect for one law—any law—is diminished, respect for all law suffers. If one of us can decide which laws we shall observe, then everybody can.

The point is that under our concept of government the emphasis has to be on massive law observance rather than massive law enforcement. We observe and try to obey the law not because we are forced to but because our respect for the rule of law overrides our private feelings. And when we come to the point that any considerable number of our citizenry have so lost the respect for the rule of law that they will deliberately defy it, either openly or clandestinely, then our whole system is in danger.

The great genius of our political structure in this country has been grounded in the capacity of the overwhelming majority of our people to accept the rule of a smaller majority. This is not to say that the majority is always right and that we may not seek to change by proper means those laws and judicial decisions with which we do not agree. But as lawyers you and I must know that the highest test of courageous and responsible citizenship lies in our willingness to obey laws that we do not like. This is the greatest expression of support that we can give to our American system of jurisprudence. It is a position that you and I have a solemn obligation to affirm as citizens but more than that as members of the Bar.

The people have a right to look to our profession for leadership in times like these. It is not enough that we acquire great skill in the trial of lawsuits and in the drafting of contracts. It is not enough that we achieve professional eminence and financial success. What is demanded of us and what our oath requires is that we use the prestige, the influence, and the knowledge of our profession to give direction to our state and nation in times of crisis.

In the past I am sorry to say that too many of us here in Mississippi have not asserted the leadership that we were capable of in times of confusion and crisis. Too many of us lawyers have sat on our hands and by our silence and acquiescence have lent our support to positions that from a legal standpoint, if indeed not from a moral and ethical standpoint, have been patently wrong. We do our state and country no service—we do not advance the cause of responsible government—we add no luster to our profession, when as lawyers we permit to go unchallenged the irresponsible and demagogic attacks from both the far left and the far right on our system of justice.

—"Our Duty to the Law," speech, Hinds County Bar Association, Jackson, Mississippi, 1965.

I do not consider this low reputation of the legal profession justified. I think we can say that it is based, to some extent, on a lack of public understanding of the lawyer's role—a role that is frequently unpopular. It is based on a misunderstanding of the concept of the adversary system of settling controversies. It is based on a lack of appreciation of the duty of the lawyer to represent unpopular clients and unpopular causes. It is based on a failure to comprehend the complex processes that frequently are involved in the attainment of results in the profession. We suffer from the onus that attaches to increased governmental laws and regulations. We are blamed unnecessarily many times for the length of time it takes to achieve a just result. Having stated these problems, I hasten to add further that we must apply our best abilities to mitigate the effects of them, and in the process, we must never lose sight of our responsibility to maintain a system that provides legal services—adequate legal services—to everyone at reasonable cost.

. . . When I mention ethics, I am not talking about those offenses for which one can be disbarred. I am not talking about the things you can go to jail for. I am talking about those more subtle and less visible failings which we see too much of in the day-to-day practice of law. I am talking about, for example, the subtle and undisclosed conflicts of interest, the failure to advise clients adequately and fully, the shading of testimony and the withholding of facts that should be disclosed, and the abuse of the legal process in many other ways to abort rather than to secure a just and proper result. More often than not these unfortunate results are based on two fundamental weaknesses—a gross and overriding concern for financial gain at any price, and a need to compensate for an inadequate knowledge of the law. What is really involved here is a need to understand that unique nature of the legal profession. It must be always regarded as more than a mere way to make a living. It must be regarded as more than a technical trade.

. . . If we are to reduce the cynicism which exists about our profession, we shall do so only by the example of our performance. This is a performance that extends to the privilege of providing wise and unselfish leadership in the solving of the problems of our community, our state and our nation. We must remember that it will not be enough that we are good lawyers. We must also be good citizens. So while we work to improve our profession from within, we also must understand that we

have an inescapable duty to our profession and to our society to
make life more humane and more decent for our fellow man.

—Commencement address, University of Mississippi Law School, August 14, 1978.

While some may complain of a society with too many laws and
too many lawyers, it is obvious that a society without a strong
and stable system of jurisprudence would immediately degenerate into chaos and anarchy.

. . . The first test of worthiness to be a lawyer is to be willing and to be able to do good work. If our clients are not better
off for our having served them, then we ought to take down our
shingle. And we do not need to render our clients more service
than they need.

. . . Lawyers have a continuing responsibility to make the
legal system in which we function work better. That system
has been largely fashioned by us, and if some parts of it do not
perform well, it is up to us to fix it. To many ordinary citizens
and, for that matter, to most of us lawyers there are times
when the wheels of justice seem to turn too slowly and too
ponderously. Without doing violence to the established rules
of due process, we must work harder at simplifying our procedures and reducing the time of judgment. That may mean that
we be willing to practice by rules that are changed to accommodate justice rather than our own interests and convenience.

. . . One of the sources of misunderstanding about our profession is based on the over-expectations as to the results we
can achieve. We have led the public to believe that for every
real or suspected wrong there is a remedy under the law, and
if there is no law, we'll make one as soon as the legislature
convenes.

. . . It may sound paradoxical but as lawyers, we must help
to reduce the litigiousness of our society if our legal system is
to function efficiently and if we are to live together as citizens
in a satisfactory manner.

. . . Let us remember that our system of justice has never pretended to be a guarantor of a perfect society—only of a reasonable society. And keeping our society reasonable is no small task these days when there are so many shrill and clamorous special interests seeking to advance their cause above all others.

. . . Let me suggest that over and above our duties and responsibilities as members of the legal profession, we have an even higher calling, because we are lawyers, to provide that essential leadership in public and community affairs that has always been a hallmark of our profession.

. . . We lawyers, of all people, must remember that we still live under a social contract in this country. We are called upon by virtue of our special training and our approach to solving problems—maybe more than any other group—to maintain that civil society that is the basis of all of our free institutions.

—Speech, Mississippi Bar Foundation, Jackson, Mississippi, February 16, 1991.

ON THE ROLE OF COURTS

Of greatest significance has been the greatly increased role of the courts in the ultimate resolution of so many of the knotty public policy and administrative questions that have defied solution at the hands of popularly elected legislative bodies. In some respects this has been a setback for our traditional system of representative government, for it is obvious that in the origins of our political structure it was never intended that the courts should serve as a substitute for the legislature in the formation of public policy. As originally conceived the role of the courts was that of arbiter and settler of disputes. In the face of the increasingly complex and politically explosive issues . . . the legislative process just has been unable or unwilling in many instances to come to grips respectively with the problems that have confronted us on so many fronts. It is an unhappy and unfortunate commentary on the times in which we live that we have seen the courts move into positions which they would not have assumed a generation ago—simply because no one else wanted to bite the bullet. One of the unspoken attitudes prevalent in many a state legislative chamber is the resigned assurance that if a statutory remedy for a sticky issue cannot be achieved, then relief is always available in the courts.

The result of all of this has been to place on the courts in all too many instances responsibilities which they are not really equipped to assume. For the ultimate answer is not automatically achieved when the judges deliver their opinion. In most cases—and in direct proportion to the difficulty and complexity of the issue being decided—there must follow the tortuous process of administrative compliance, which, again depending on the difficulty of the question, may be accompanied by a public attitude either of indifference or defiance. It remains . . . an unfortunate development that too many of these problems are being left by legislative inaction to judicial determination.

. . . The ultimate challenge facing our system of justice . . . may lie in the reform of the system itself. The inadequacy of the courts to cope with the ever-burgeoning load of cases in the major cities is already apparent to even the most casual observer. In some areas the process frequently has taken on the appearance of a factory assembly line, with defendants being herded through in a routine that makes individual judgments virtually impossible.

. . . The increasing complexity of our whole society is now creating controversies that did not exist a generation ago—controversies that are winding up in the form of lengthy, complicated lawsuits that take more and more time to be tried. We are living in a more litigious atmosphere, where grievances of every description are being brought to the courts for solution.

There is a general attitude that is beginning to pervade our society that for every ill there must be a public solution. Many persons have come to insist that our judicial processes provide a means of vindicating every wrong. But the judicial system is fast approaching its limits in terms of what it is able to do. The American people must understand . . . that there is no magic formula or public forum that is an effective substitute for individual human effort and citizen responsibility.

Moreover, the courts are now faced with an almost impossible task in being obliged to try to handle the tremendously expanded load of cases under procedures and limitations that have been inherited from a simpler time. . . . We may be at the point where we need to rethink what constitutes crime and whether we need to clutter our courts with so-called criminal cases that might better be handled in other ways.

. . . The very nature of the judiciary is such that it calls for the very best people that our society can produce. We have had many men and women of unusual dedication and ability serving there, but in too many instances we have let inadequate and temperamentally unfit leadership find places on the bench.

It is hoped that in the future we will see a resumption of a greater degree of reliance on legislative bodies at all levels for the solutions to our major social problems so that the courts can go back to their original roles as the settlers of disputes.

. . . It is . . . our God-given right in this free society in which we live to decide for ourselves the degree of discipline and self-restraint that we shall impose upon ourselves. Having now come so far down the path toward the achievement of tolerance and understanding and compassion, let us understand that we cannot expect that any system of justice can deliver to each of us relief from all of our problems. We must learn then to moderate our demands as to what we expect from our government and lessen our insistence on instant public solutions for our private ills. Our system of justice has never pretended to nor can it ever be a guarantor of a perfect society. It can only try to be the imperfect conservator of our collective hopes and dreams. . . . Those hopes and dreams must include our continued commitment to the recognition of the inherent worth and dignity of every person. Only as we seek it for the weakest of our fellow citizens can we assure a decent and just society for ourselves.

—Speech, Virginia Polytechnic Institute and State University, December 6, 1978.

ON PRISONS

In several states of the Deep South there have been continuing efforts over many years to eliminate some of the dehumanizing practices that have served to confirm criminal behavior rather than to rehabilitate people. This has been a slow and uncertain process, however; too slow in fact for many of the federal judges, who, in some instances as in Mississippi and Alabama, have stepped into a major administrative role in determining to a very specific degree what is acceptable and unacceptable.

. . . This has brought the courts into sharp conflict at times with state legislatures and other state government officials, but in the final analysis the result has been to bring substantial change to the region's prisons and an increased sensitivity of citizens to the antiquated and inadequate facilities that have for too long remained outside the public conscience. While some progress was being made independent of judicial action, no one can seriously doubt that the impetus of the court decisions has been the driving force behind most of the changes that have taken place—changes that now most responsible persons would admit needed to be made. Again it is unfortunate that such changes have had to be achieved through judicial edicts and at the expense of weakening local autonomy and control.

—Speech, Virginia Polytechnic Institute and State University, December 6, 1978.

Of all of the multitude of problems that public officials are called on to deal with none is more thankless than that of overseeing the prison system. There are no alumni associations to marshal support—no final graduations.

... The greatest deterrent to crime has proven to be an understanding by lawbreakers that punishment will be swift and sure for their crime. It also needs to be as uniform as possible. Let punishment for most nonviolent property-related crimes take the form of supervised public service work in the community and restitution for the victims of the crime. ... It would ensure that we then had enough space behind bars to keep those real criminals who are a menace to the lives and safety of law-abiding citizens.

—Television commentary, WJTV, Jackson, Mississippi, 1985.

ON JUSTICE IN THE SOUTH

It is my conviction that an overwhelming majority of the people in this country—South and North—are and always have been committed to a system of fairness in the administration of justice. This has been too often a concept that has existed in the abstract but that has failed under the prejudices, tensions, and weaknesses of actual situations and events. The South has presented the most striking paradox in this regard. Here we have a region whose people have been noted for their reverence of and respect for the visible signs and symbols of civil authority—the Constitution, the pledge of allegiance, the flag. We have been among the first to deplore attacks on our system of government and the first to volunteer in its defense. We have been sturdy exponents of faith in the ultimate triumph of right over wrong in an obviously imperfect world, where ideals like equality and universal justice remain far from reality. The trouble is that historically in the South we have often labored under a system of justice that was based more on social mores than legal standards. Without always being conscious of the injustice of it, for many years we condoned an approach to the administration of justice that reflected in its most favorable application a benign paternalism and in its worst form a heinous and cynical disregard for fundamental human rights.

. . . Actually what we are observing in all areas of . . . judicial administration in the South is a process that is eliminating most of the distinctions between our section and the rest of the country. A generation ago . . . there was the generally accepted system under which obviously different standards of justice prevailed. It was newsworthy when a white defendant was convicted, as occasionally happened, of a crime against a black victim. On the other hand, strict and frequently harsh sentences were usually meted out when the situation was reversed. And . . . a third standard of justice—usually more lenient— occurred when a defendant and victim were both black. All of this . . . represented a sometimes bizarre and always interesting journey through the thicket of Southern mores. It was a mixture . . . of benign paternalism and a callous disregard for human dignity, and the result was for a long time a kind of judicial schizophrenia where our professions of justice were not always matched by actual results. We can be grateful that most of this dual system of judging has gone the way of the one-mule sharecropper and the commissary store.

—Speech, Virginia Polytechnic Institute and State University, December 6, 1978.

This may be a good time to look at where we stand in this part of the country at this stage of our age-old battles with terror. Most of us . . . do not have to search our memories too far to recall how the Deep South was for so long the scene of unspeakable terroristic acts. At the risk of digging up some old ghosts that some folks will undoubtedly say should better lie unremembered, let me remind you of how we succumbed to the notion that the Southern way of life . . . the segregated way of life, had to be defended at all costs. We invoked all sorts of emotional arguments to try to close our eyes to the obvious injustice of it all.

Those sanctions were not always imposed at the point of a gun or the threat of a hangman's noose. They were imposed quietly and subtly in many instances, but the damage to our democratic ideals was just as pervasive.

Take such a basic constitutional right as voting for example. I can remember as a young, perhaps unduly naive, state legislator in 1948 sitting on the front porch of the modest president's home at what was then called Alcorn A&M College and having him tell me of his despair in not being permitted to register to vote at the county seat of the county where his school was located. Here was a man holding a Ph.D. degree from a major university who was denied the right to vote. There was no direct physical threat made to him, but the message was clear. One did not tamper with the local mores. Democracy had its limits.

That was how the system defended itself at the white-collar level. On the lower socioeconomic scale, the results were harsh beyond our imagining.

. . . Now we are beginning to come to terms with our responsibility to right the old wrongs. The truth is that for so long we were really all in bondage—white folks to their fears of change—black folks the victims of those fears. And the democratic ideals on which this country was founded suffered grievous wounds. Democracy cannot thrive in the face of unreasoning fear and mindless intimidation.

—Speech, Mississippi Political Service Association, Delta State University, February 27, 2003.

ON TERRORISM AND THE
PROTECTION OF LIBERTIES

It is a long recognized axiom that democratic ideals are most imperiled when the people of a democracy are most frightened and insecure. It is then that we tend to look for protection from those forces, real or imagined, that we most fear. Many political leaders in the past understood this and often used these fears to accomplish their political ends. Some of those fears have been justified, and the motives of many political leaders to respond to those fears have been sincere.

The two most notable examples of legitimately based fears and the responses thereto have . . . been Pearl Harbor and the September 11th World Trade Center horror. One of the results in the first instance was an assault on individual liberties that caused this country to force loyal Americans who happened to be of Japanese descent into internment camps. There were few protests from the citizens of our beleaguered country.

Again following the events of 9–11, we passed the so-called Patriot Act and began the surveillance and apprehension of many residents of this country, many of them American citizens, simply because of their national origin or what they looked like. While so far those developments may not represent a major assault on our liberties and freedoms, I do think they call for a careful assessment of where the proper boundaries of such efforts should lie.

Even though we have been recently victimized by a shocking kind of terror, we cannot afford to develop a careless or indifferent or intimidated acquiescence in the further extension of intrusive searches, seizures, and surveillance. . . . Legitimate national defense is one thing. Unnecessary snooping into the private lives of American citizens is something else.

. . . It is easy to justify excesses in the name of patriotism and national defense. I remember only too well the hysteria

that accompanied the early years of the Cold War. There were
some well-meaning individuals who saw a Communist behind
every bush. There were many unscrupulous politicians who
trafficked in this hysteria. Perhaps the most infamous was
Senator Joe McCarthy, who for several years intimidated some
of the country's most powerful leaders. . . . We Mississippians
can take pride in the fact that it was our Senator John Stennis
who finally called McCarthy's hand and set in motion his ultimate demise.

The Cold War subjected this country to the long and dark
threat of the terror of total annihilation. I can remember the
school drills in preparation for that terrible day when the bomb
might drop. I can remember some of my friends building bomb
shelters in their backyards. The threat of terror was very real.
That threat has now reemerged in a more sinister and less
certain form. We have a right to be concerned. We do not have
a right to diminish our commitment to the maintenance of
our individual liberties. If we do, then the terrorists will have
done far more damage to our country than the mad bombers
did on 9–11.

. . . These are perilous times. The threat of terror is real.
But a greater threat is to let our insecurity cause us to retreat
into our little social and ethnic enclaves living in suspicion of
our neighbors and our neighbors living in fear of us. We have
come too far in this country in breaking down the old barriers
that once separated us to start erecting new barriers.

—Speech, Mississippi Political Service Association, Delta State University, February 27, 2003.

CIVIC
RESPONSIBILITY

Dedication ceremony of the William F. Winter Archives and
History Building in Jackson, Mississippi, November 2003.

ON THE RESPONSIBLE JOURNALIST

In a calmer, simpler time both the freewheeling sensation-seller and the timid time-server could represent the journalistic profession without doing damage to the body politic. Now, in our increasingly urbanized and diverse society where the very massiveness of information frustrates and confuses us all, we are totally dependent on the skill and integrity of a relatively small number of men and women to select and tell us what we shall know about the events of this world in which we live.

The relevance of this is pointed up in the swirl of events around us in our own community at this very hour with all of the conflicts and contradictions that they portend. And because so many of our people are not able to comprehend clearly what all these things mean emphasizes even more the necessity for the most articulate and interpretative reporting that we can get.

Few events ever hold clear and decisive meaning at the time that they happen, but the discerning reporter has to have that sixth sense that enables him to see them in their proper relation to the unending pattern of human striving and human conflict that somehow does take shape in the long sweep of history. The reporter then, in effect, is the instant historian, selecting that which must be recorded almost as fast as it happens, without the benefit of either conference or contemplation.

He does not have the advantage of a hundred years of elapsed time between the event and the writing, with all of the wonderful opportunity that such a time lag affords for romantic innovation. He more often has a deadline of thirty minutes.

There are few institutions about whose role so much confusion seems to exist as that of the press. . . . Men have debated for years about what the role of the press in a free society ought to be. Some have held that it has no higher purpose than to mirror and defend the way of life, good or bad, strong or weak, of the community in which it functions. Others argue that the press is like any other business operation—that its principal task is to return a profit to its owners. There are still others who feel that the press should not attempt to exercise any discretion, moral or otherwise, on the range of matters which it presents.

In my opinion none of these concepts carries out the essential function which the press must perform if it is to be worthy of the special status that it occupies in our political and economic system. It was not an idle grant of privilege that was incorporated in our Constitution in the First Amendment. This guarantee of the freedom of the press automatically implies the highest measure of public responsibility.

For only a responsible press can hope to remain free. The 1947 report of the Commission on Freedom of the Press contained this blunt warning: "No democracy will indefinitely tolerate concentration of private power, irresponsible and strong enough to thwart the democratic aspirations of the people. If these giant agencies of communication are irresponsible, not even the First Amendment will protect their freedom from government control. The Amendment will be amended."

. . . Only so long as conscientious individual reporters, sensitive to their primary duty to their reader rather than their publisher or their managing editor, insist on first getting the news that the public needs to know and then on getting it in their papers where it can be read, will a free press as we understand it be capable or for that matter be worthy of being maintained.

. . . It is an old axiom that great reporters make great newspapers, but by the same token only great newspapers can keep great reporters. And they do this by believing in them and more tangibly by printing their stories.

Clifton Daniel of the *New York Times* has defined journalism as a calling—not a trade or profession. And he thinks that every journalist must live by the standards of that calling—standards that are not subject to change by the shifting winds of public taste or political expediency.

The duty of the reporter under this concept then is that vital one to do for the citizen what he does not have the time or the ability to do for himself. He not only must gather the information, but he must decide what is worth gathering. He not only has to be the eyes and ears of our society, but he must form a part of its conscience, too.

What I am saying is that it is not enough that he spell correctly and get the names right. He also has the practical and difficult job of deciding how much to tell the people and what is worth telling them. There are no guidelines here, and it is in this area that the true worth and integrity of a reporter is determined. He will encounter situations where no one else but him can report certain facts.

These must be lonely and agonizing times for the conscientious journalist in measuring just what his responsibility is. There are no textbooks in the schools of journalism, and there are no rule books in the newsroom that answer these questions. There is nothing but the integrity and the conscience of the reporter.

There are some people who think that the public interest is served by not calling attention to acts of public infidelity to duty, by not reporting acts of injustice, by not citing situations that might embarrass those in positions of authority. Too many times we have seen conscientious newspapermen fall victim to this idea in their understandable desire to get along and be known by everybody as a "good fellow." . . . But I do insist that a good reporter can't be concerned about what toes he may step on or whose feeling he may ruffle in his honest, sincere efforts to get the facts to the public. I am not advocating muck-raking either. A good reporter would rather report the good news than the bad, but more than that he will insist on writing the truth.

. . . A free society can progress only as it has access to and makes decisions based on the real facts about itself. I have no doubt about the ability of a people to function effectively and to govern themselves properly so long as they are enabled to know what the true issues are.

But in a day of Madison Avenue artificiality, of image-making, of mimeographed double-talk that passes for press releases, of carefully structured press conferences, of closed public meetings, of deliberate efforts on the part of many in the political and business world to confuse the people, the conscientious reporter has a special responsibility of making certain that he is not one of the actors—that he is not just a cog in the image-making apparatus. There is nothing that makes a reporter's job easier than the ready-to-print handout. There is nothing so corrupting as to rely on them.

Of even greater cause for concern is the technique that is widespread in some quarters of deliberately masking editorial opinion under the guise of straight news. . . . It is a debauching of a free press for a partisan columnist to masquerade as an objective news reporter. And nothing will do greater damage to the institution of responsible journalism than this practice of camouflaging editorials under a news story head and a reporter's byline.

But perhaps just as difficult as objectively reporting the news is the role of the good reporter in getting society to understand what he is doing in filing his story in the first place. Not only does he have the duty of protecting us from the ready acceptance of the easy half-truth but he has the more complex task of getting us to grasp the reality of the hard whole-truth.

Accustomed to listening only to those voices that have told us what we have wanted to hear, we have been moved to reject as those of our enemy those voices that pointed up what we have not wanted to hear. Some of us have not been willing to open our ears to what have frequently been facts that we did not choose to be reminded of.

. . . The only journey worth taking is that endless one in search of truth. . . . The best antidote for false witness is the straight story. And we who have from time to time felt unfairly put upon by some who would distort our manners and our motives should take reassurance that honest reporting brings its own reward. We must understand that if what we purport to believe and stand for will not bear exposure in the bright light of a reporter's honest reporting, it is probably not worth defending in the first place.

It will be from this vantage point that the great break-through in understanding among men will be made and the cause of decency and honor served. We shall progress as a free people only as we share a common desire to have the truth presented to us. This, of itself, can be a rewarding and maturing experience for many of us whose minds have been closed tight and who have adopted the old adage, "Don't confuse me with the facts."

Perhaps this is why there are those who are suspicious of a press that is truly free. It can be a painful process, under the impact of reality, to be required to reevaluate our positions and to defend them if we can. But this is one of the great contributions that reporters . . . make in requiring us all "to look at the record." . . . More of us need to understand, too, that the honest, imaginative reporter holds out the ability to us to get a true vision of the kind of society that we are capable of achieving.

Instead of reacting with anger to honest reporting of injustice, more of us ought to respond with a demand that the injustice be ended. Instead of reacting with hostility at sincere efforts to call attention to inefficiency in government, more of us ought to be concerned with reducing the inefficiency. Instead of feeling betrayed by a suggestion that there are areas where the quality of law-enforcement might be improved, more of us need to see to it that it is improved.

Only in this way can our society achieve for itself the golden promise that it has the capacity to attain. The conscientious reporter can be our mirror to point up our faults, but more than that he can be our beacon to show us our goal.

—"The Responsible Journalist in a Free Society," speech, Bill Minor Dinner, Heidelberg Hotel, Jackson, Mississippi, June 25, 1966.

ON COMMUNITY BUILDING

There must be a recognition that we still live under a social contract in this country. In spite of the progress that we have made, there are still too many people who are getting left out. . . . We must work at the elimination of the remaining barriers that divide us as a people. Having largely demolished the visible, tangible walls built of fear and prejudice and misguided self-interest that kept us apart for so long, we now have not only the opportunity but the duty to make this one society.

This must involve not just a little handful of so-called do-gooders. It has to embrace the best efforts of everybody. It cannot be done cynically or grudgingly. It has to be done out of a conviction that it is right—right for us as individual citizens and right for the entire community.

—Speech, Leadership Florida, Orlando, Florida, March 24, 1990.

We are all a part of the same larger community and no single individual or program or public policy alone can solve our problems as a society. . . . We must rebuild a sense of community. We must understand that none of us is an island. The restoration of faith in our system really goes back to each one of us as individuals being willing to put more in than we take out. . . . The exclusive or even primary pursuit of our self-interest is almost a sure fire way to create a system that will ultimately break down. This . . . is at the heart of our present discontent. Too many of us have been encouraged to adopt a policy of getting while the getting was good. For some that meant taking advantage of the perquisites of public office. But for too many of us ordinary citizens it meant claiming all the benefits that the system could make available whether we paid for them or not. Political self-restraint and personal self-restraint went out the window together.

So it is time for all of us and especially those of us who have been so greatly favored . . . to begin to lead the return to a point of view that puts social justice before private advantage—that puts community building at least on a par with personal empire building—and that understands that our own individual liberty is inextricably linked to our respect and concern for every other individual.

—Speech, University of Texas LBJ School of Government, May 23, 1992.

It is not in the top echelons of business or politics or the professions that the broadest opportunity for effective leadership lies. The greatest challenge lies in this process of community building. I am convinced that the source of our most urgent need and our highest satisfaction lies in the strengthening of the individual communities in which we live. . . . It is here that we establish the relationships with our neighbors and reaffirm our mutual interdependence. It is here that we have the best chance to create the structures that make life better for everyone.

. . . As never before in our history we are called upon to sustain and expand our commitment to building up the communities where we live. We must understand how much more we have to do. For unless we continue to work to bridge the fault lines of race and class and educational and financial disparity that still divide us, we can never expect to reach our true potential as a nation.

—"Leadership and Ethics," speech, Kellogg Foundation, New Orleans, Louisiana, February 22, 2000.

ON ECONOMIC DEVELOPMENT

It is now virtually impossible for the South to outbid the labor-rich countries of the third world or even, for that matter, the newly competitive other sections of our own country. What we can do and must do . . . is to sell our strengths, of which we have many, without giving away the store. Those attributes . . . are climate, access to markets, honest and responsible political leadership, a confirmed work ethic, a commitment to quality education, and a reliable infrastructure. The states and communities that aggressively promote economic development on that basis will do all right in the years ahead.

—Television commentary, WJTV, Jackson, Mississippi, 1985.

In spite of the considerable progress that we have made in educational achievement as a result of various reforms in the 1980s, we are confronted with a more difficult set of problems than we have known before. Faced with the most competitive, demanding, globally involved challenge in our history, we are still not producing the number of skilled workers that will enable us to be competitive in a global economy. We are in a contest now to see which country can make the best use of its human resources.

. . . Our underdeveloped human capital remains our greatest barrier to economic growth and prosperity. The plain fact is that as long as we have so many undereducated people, our state and region are going to be poorer than the rest of the country. Poorly educated people translate into poor people. Education is the only thing that will break the cycle of poverty. It is the only thing that will unlock the door to economic opportunity.

. . . Why has our region ranked so low in per capita income? It is certainly not because we are lacking in natural resources. By anybody's standards this is a naturally rich area—productive land, abundant energy and minerals, bountiful timber, plenty of water, clean air. It is poor because we have too many underproductive people. Put in plain, hardheaded economic terms, it is not just a zero to our economy to have so many undereducated people. It is a minus. The more undereducated people our region has, the poorer it is. Because they are undereducated, they can't carry their share of the burden. They are the people who have to be carried.

—"What Are the Real Costs of the South's Poor Educational System?" speech, Rotary Club and Women's Network, Birmingham, Alabama, February 15, 1989.

Community economic development almost always depends on the existence of local indigenous entrepreneurs—businessmen and women who have a stake in the community and who are not just passing through on the way to make a fast buck and then go somewhere else.

The communities that will have the soundest prospects for growth in the future will be those where a strong local entrepreneurial spirit prevails—where relatively small, diverse locally-owned businesses continue to thrive and do well. This spirit is often stimulated by negative forces. The hard times in some of the traditional industries may encourage more people to pursue their own creative business ideas and become self-employed.

—"The Revival of Rural America," speech, Rural Development Conference, Birmingham, Alabama, February 1986.

We have to break out of the "good ole boy" network in terms of deal-making. There has to be an opening up of our informal business practices in ways that will give women and minorities an even playing field. So often it is at civic club luncheons and other similar gatherings that significant business is transacted. Women and minorities, not being much in evidence at such meetings, are frequently the last to know about business opportunities. That needs to change.

The kind of communities and the kind of country that are going to be able to compete in the global market places of the future will be shaped by leaders emerging from the ranks of women and minorities. The quality of that leadership will be determined by the vision which we impart to this generation of young Southerners and young Americans.

It can be a vision based on bitterness and despair and greed and rejection with all of the negative implications which that would hold for our nation. Or, on the other hand, with the encouragement and inspiration and understanding of more of us and our so-called successful colleagues in business . . . it can be a vision based on the building of a freer, more just and more rewarding society for everyone—where we stop to help pick up those who may stumble along the way and where nobody gets left out.

—"Moving Minorities from Despair to Hope," speech, Workforce Diversity Conference, Atlanta, Georgia, June 26, 1990.

ON FARMERS

Having grown up on a farm which I still own, I have long been aware of the uncertainties of farming as a means of livelihood. As a matter of fact, I have observed from time to time that I chose politics over farming as a more secure career. For many a small farmer, the writing is on the wall clearer than ever that he can't afford to keep on farming. It should be pointed out that the farmer is the one seller in the marketplace who has practically no voice in what he gets for his products.

—Television commentary, WJTV, Jackson, Mississippi, 1985.

Since we shall remain a state which will be a major source of agricultural production, it is imperative that we create an economic basis that makes the farmer competitive in the marketplace. Surely this can be done without totally abandoning our farms to massive corporate developments. One answer obviously lies in gaining for the producers of agricultural products more influence in the setting of prices for what they grow. A system of industry wide marketing cooperatives that would be capable of helping to establish for an entire crop an effective price may ultimately be an answer to a problem that has plagued farmers from earliest times.

—"The Ultimate Legacy," chapter in *Mississippi 1990*, published by University Press of Mississippi, 1979.

The farm adjoined our place on the west. It was an early New Deal project to relocate down-and-out white sharecroppers. Some people disparagingly called it the "bull farm," because of an initial report that oxen rather than mules would be used as work animals. The Farm Security Administration served as landlord. The tenants would sharecrop for the government. It was a noble experiment in attempting to lift out of total economic disaster these down-on-their-luck farmers who bore proud Anglo-Saxon names and who had worked hard and honorably all their lives. But a willingness to work was not enough in those bleak years of the great depression.

. . . They inherited the rundown farm cabins as their living quarters and worked the fields along the river. If there was an element of hopelessness about them, I was never aware of it. I of course did not recognize them for what they were—a part of that massive army of twenty to thirty million displaced Americans for whom the early 1930s was one long nightmare of deprivation. But for these long-suffering cotton farmers there had never been enough to go around—not enough education or health care or dignity—certainly not enough money.

—Unpublished personal memoirs.

ON THE FUTURE

I can tell you that in spite of all of the problems, real and imagined, that seem to plague us, these are good times—maybe the best. If it seems that they are not, it is largely because we have forgotten the pain and sacrifice and the effort that have brought us to where we are. And so instead of living in mindless pessimism and self-centered discontent, let us turn with enthusiasm and excitement to the unfinished work of building a fairer and more compassionate society and be thankful that we can have a hand in that noble task.

—Remarks, Renaissance Weekend, Hilton Head Island, South Carolina, 1994.

ON CIVIC RESPONSIBILITY

The problem of providing decent leadership for our people is not that our leaders don't know better. It is that they don't act better. So more than idealism and maturity and wisdom are involved here, and as important as these qualities are in the make-up of the responsible citizen, they avail nothing without the element of courage that is necessary to uphold noble ideas and put them into action.

This has been one of our problems in recent years here in Mississippi where we have permitted a lot of people to go around in the name of patriotism or tradition or some other noble cause and tell the people many things that weren't so. And too many of us sat back and allowed ourselves to be persuaded that maybe we did enjoy some immunity from obeying laws that we didn't like or didn't agree with. But responsible citizenship calls for the exercise of the best qualities of mind and heart that we have, and now we know that there is no such easy answer.

—"The Meaning of Responsible Citizenship," speech delivered to students at the University of Mississippi, February 23, 1965.

We must understand that there is no permanent, unchanging, monolithic body of public opinion that freezes forever positions on most public issues. . . . It would seem that there is nothing more volatile or impermanent than public opinion on almost any given issue.

. . . At a time when so many narrowly focused special interest groups abound, we should consider ourselves as lobbyists for the public interest—as petitioners for the people. We must be involved in creating constituencies for quality education, for the preservation of a good environment, for the formation of more responsive structures of government, and we must remember that our constituencies are primarily formed at the local level.

. . . We must bring together diverse constituencies. We must be a bridge between people and groups representing different interests but who have more in common than they know about. We must help break down the barriers that separate rural and urban people—blacks and whites and other nationalities—the young and the old—the affluent and the non-affluent.

This nation must never permit itself to be divided permanently into two societies each alien to the other—one defending blindly its privilege and the other fighting desperately for its rights. There is room enough in this broad, rich land to accommodate the legitimate needs and aspirations of everyone. Our task is to help that ideal become a reality.

. . . A responsibility that is ours is to help communities to identify their local strengths and resources. Too often we sit around in the places where we live waiting for something to happen—waiting for some goodies to fall out of the sky or at least to fall out of Washington—without recognizing the untapped resources that are available to us where we are.

This often is a matter of stimulating vision where none has existed—of creating, educating, informing and building community leadership. Helping to establish models of things that work—sharing common vision, transmitting a spark of know-how—continue to be our tasks.

All of this calls for a continuing process of self-education and an education of our fellow citizens. This must be true education—not in sound-bites and slogans and superficialities but in a better understanding of the gravity of our decisions in the preservation and perpetuation of a free society.

—Speech, National Civic League, Charlotte, North Carolina, November 12, 1988.

In spite of the considerable progress that we have made, especially here in this part of the country in the last twenty-five years, in removing the legal barriers to opportunity, many extralegal barriers remain. These are the more pervasive, more difficult barriers to remove. These are barriers that, nevertheless, enslave and condemn people in a free land to lead lives of wretchedness and despair. These are the prisons fashioned of ignorance and drug abuse and a family structure that is falling apart. These are problems that tear at the very fabric of a civilized society and threaten our future.

In this great, rich land we must understand that none of us is really free of the bondage of ignorance and poverty and neglect until all are free. There is more than a humanitarian or ethical dimension to this. It is also a matter of self-interest that we do not degenerate into a society where we live behind walls in fear of our neighbors and our neighbors live in distrust of us. We must not permit ourselves to be divided into two groups of people—one affluent, prospering, and unconcerned—the other poor, ignorant, and in despair.

It does not have to be that way, and it will not be that way if enough of us . . . resolve that it does not happen. Asserting in a more positive and aggressive way our traditional role of civic and community leadership will make the difference in determining how orderly and just a society we shall pass on to our children.

—Speech, Mississippi Bar Foundation, February 16, 1991.

One of the reasons that more young people do not commit themselves to larger social and political objectives is that they do not know enough about our tradition of community that was a part of a simpler age. Turned off by the ambiguities of our modern culture, they frequently retreat into the shell of their own narrow interests or they on the other hand forfeit their individuality to the seductive call of a mindless conformity.

Unfortunately we have not done a very effective job of educating people in how to achieve the right balance. . . . That is a task in which we must all be engaged—parents, teachers, civic and community leaders, foundations, and particularly the great liberal arts institutions.

There does not seem to be enough of this kind of instruction going on these days—particularly in the area of civic education. Because of the increasing diversity of our citizenry it is getting more difficult to agree on what to teach in our schools, as witness the recent controversy over what our history books ought to contain. But just because we are a less homogenous people than we used to be does not make less important the task of teaching students the nature of civic responsibility and an understanding of our civil society. In fact, it is more vital

than ever that in the face of those changing cultural values
there be an increased instruction in civic participation and
community building.

. . . When I speak of civic education, I am not talking about a
narrow, dogmatic, sanctimonious kind of teaching that suggests
arbitrary and simplistic solutions to very complicated problems, and I am not talking about some sort of sterile national
curriculum. I am talking about the communication of a vision
that makes us dissatisfied with a status quo of easy accommodation and self-gratification. I am talking about the transmission of an understanding of responsible modes of behavior that
enable us to live in harmony with our neighbors, our families
and ourselves. It is, to put it simply, education for the office of
citizen. It is an education that has as its center a recognition
of the worth and dignity of every human being. It is a commitment that we put more into our society than we take out.
It is an understanding that each generation must bring a new
and fresh vitality to the process of renewing and reviving and
expanding the values that maintain our stability as a people.

. . . In our country it has been this element of community
building through the engagement of civic and humanitarian
and educational institutions that has maintained our stability as a nation. I believe that this was really the force, stronger
than the military factor, that was the decisive element in the
long struggle with the cynical forces of communism. We were
able to create socially responsible public capital and build a
sense of community that made the ultimate difference.

—Speech, Davidson College, October 26, 1996.

The most important office is that of citizen. It is the office that
transmits all political authority.

Only through the collective judgment of private citizens,
acting through their elected agents, are the public decisions
made that affect the ultimate quality of our lives. Unfortunately

too few of us take that office of citizen seriously enough. Too few of us choose to exercise the power that goes with that office. Too many of us do not bother to vote or to participate in the process of deciding vital public policy—of what kind of schools we shall have, of the quality of the environment in which we live, or the future of our most treasured institutions.

Therein lies the potential for our greatest peril. . . . The gravest danger may lie in letting ourselves be overwhelmed by fear or suspicion or apathy or cynicism; by putting our petty self-serving personal interests ahead of community building; by making the question, "What's in it for me?" our principal concern; in short by forgetting about that contract that we have with each other.

. . . If we become a society riven by race and class where the gap between the rich and the poor continues to widen, we shall pay a huge penalty in the quality of our lives and the stability of our country in the future.

A democratic society cannot leave these problems to be solved by blind chance or individual impulse. We must work at it together. We must have a shared vision that recognizes our mutual obligation. It is a vision that must be transmitted to others.

All of us must work at helping create more knowledgeable and informed public opinion that will be able to stand up to the demagogues and the political hucksters. . . . That is how you pay your dues for the privilege . . . of living in a free society.

—Found in writings for a possible commencement address in 2003.

ON DIVERSITY

Racial diversity in schools can reap great benefits. First, a racially diverse student body can improve teaching and learning by exposing students to different perspectives and experiences.

Persons of different races often have different cultural backgrounds. They also often have different experiences in the world and, in turn, often view the world differently. Imagine studying such topics as the Civil War, the proper role of law enforcement in society, or the U.S. Constitution in a racially homogenous environment. Clearly we learn more when we all learn together.

. . . A racially diverse student body can enhance civic values by bringing children together to interact as equals and to learn the values of understanding, tolerance, and respect for others that can make all students better citizens. The evidence indicates that racially diverse schools can structure activities to promote positive interracial interactions and that such interactions can promote racial tolerance and trust. And these improved race relations in school can continue throughout life. Students who attend desegregated schools are more likely to live in racially diverse neighborhoods and to have friends from other racial backgrounds. Thus, racially diverse and integrated schools not only can yield smarter, better-adjusted students, but they can help us become One America.

—"The Desegregation of America's Schools: A Dream Unrealized," speech, Little Rock, Arkansas, September 26, 1997.

To an increasing extent all of us will be living in a world of diversity. America is rapidly becoming the most racially diverse country on the planet. No one can lead who does not understand and appreciate that diversity. We have to learn how to get along with other people whose culture and background and religion and color are different than our own.

. . . Working to eliminate the remaining vestiges of racism in this increasingly diverse country is a goal that is absolutely essential to our well-being as a nation.

—"Leadership and Ethics," speech, Kellogg Foundation, New Orleans, Louisiana, February 22, 2000.

ON RACE AND RACIAL RECONCILIATION

Other solutions must be found for the ever-present problems of race relations than the bull-whip and the shotgun. It is my observation that very few mobs ever spontaneously and automatically form. But regardless of what motivates unthinking men to take the law into their own hands, it is the clear and unmistakable duty of Southern politicians to see to it that it does not happen. And this duty extends not just to the dispersal of mobs once they have formed but to the deliberate and calculated avoidance of any statements or actions that would lend to incite their formation in the first place.

Our political leadership must appeal to the best that is in us—not the worst; to our higher selves not our baser instincts. Only in this way can our section diminish some of the tensions that have already caused us so much grief and even now threaten more. This is no time to be drinking from the wells of bitterness and recrimination. The political leader who can successfully turn his people from a preoccupation with the race issue and all of the supercharged emotions of anxiety, fear, and hate which that issue suggests, will, in my opinion, have served well the cause of Southern statesmanship and helped to put his region on the road to a happier and better day.

—"The Problems of Southern Politics," speech, All Saints' Junior College, Vicksburg, Mississippi, March 27, 1963.

Because the racial make-up of this country is changing so drastically, all of us have to work harder than ever to overcome the fault line of race.

. . . It is obvious that our capacity to exist as a great nation in the future will depend on how well we avoid an economic and educational stratification of our citizenry based on race. We must learn to live together and to be united by shared values. A beginning point in this process may be a simple recognition that we do not and probably cannot see a great many issues from the same perspective. How far we think we have come in race relations depends largely on where we stand. Most white people think we have come further than most black people think we have. But one thing we can agree on is the proposition that we must provide an opportunity to every person regardless of race or class to secure a competitive education which will lead to a more rewarding economic future. These are the elements around which we must come together.

. . . What I also believe we can agree on and unite behind is the proposition that racial prejudice and racist speech and action must be considered outside the bounds of acceptable conduct in our society; that the elimination of the remaining areas of racial injustice must be a matter of individual commitment as well as national priority; and that we must work to improve and hopefully to eliminate the social conditions that contribute to unequal opportunities.

—"From the Ivory Tower to the Mean Streets: Higher Education's Role in Community Building," speech, Tufts University, June 12, 1998.

All of us, black and white, fall victim to stereotypes. Without knowing who somebody else is, we form judgments based on what we imagine or think we know rather than what we really know about them.

These stereotypes come in all kinds of hurtful forms. And we can all be victims. I have found how difficult it is for us in Mississippi to overcome the old negative stereotypes of the past. I never cease to be amazed at the number of people in other parts of the country who seem to have an image of this state frozen in the sixties.

. . . The stereotyping between races is particularly hard to remove. Opinion polls show how far the gap is between fact and imagination especially when people have little association with each other. So many black people have the view that most white people are racists. So many white people have the view that black people are inferior. Those opinions are usually formed on the basis of the most superficial observation or on the basis of deliberate distortion of the truth.

Maybe the hardest thing for us white folks to recognize is the fact that because we are white we enjoy a certain privilege based on our skin color. While most of us whites . . . have had to work hard to achieve whatever we have done, at least we didn't have to face the ever-present uncertainty of acceptance based on our skin color, and we have been able to move easily in and through the informal networks that lead to social and financial success. We really can't know what discrimination is like until we have walked in another's shoes. Now that we have come so far from the old days of blatant racial discrimination, let us understand that we still have a lot left to do. There are still many situations that black people confront every day that make them realize that all the barriers are not down.

But having said that, let me also say that the cause of improved race relations is not served by having the issue of race used by blacks as a crutch or an excuse. Invoking the cry of race prejudice to cover up an undesirable situation is just as wrong as race prejudice itself. All of this is a matter of trying to be honest with ourselves and each other. It is a matter of developing a sense of trust based on everybody—black and white— trying to start from the same place. That is admittedly harder for blacks to do than for whites. For blacks have more to forgive even if they cannot and probably should not forget. But there must come a time in the life of every community including our own when we must recognize that we are all in this together— when we must move past the old divisions of race and recognize our common interests and our common humanity.

. . . Communication is the antidote to prejudice.

—Speech, Rotary Club, Jackson, Mississippi, March 1, 1999.

While there is much that remains to be done to advance the cause of racial understanding in the South, it is paradoxically a measure of our progress that so few younger Southerners fully appreciate the extent of the change that has taken place.

—*Millennium Reflections*, writings completed June 15, 1999.

As a member of the President's Advisory Board on Race last year, I had the unique opportunity to look at this country as few people get to do. I went to twenty-six states and visited people of all races and ethnic backgrounds. . . . Wherever I went, irrespective of racial or cultural differences, I found that people agreed on several very basic propositions. This is what everybody agreed on: everybody wants a decent education for their children; everybody wants a fair chance to secure a job that will sustain them and their family; everybody wants to be able to live in a decent house on a safe street; everybody wants access to adequate health care; and everybody wants to be treated with dignity and respect.

Surely these are not unreasonable aspirations for people getting ready to live in the twenty-first century. Surely we can find a way to make these hopes a reality. But all of us have to be involved in achieving these results. We can't just leave it to the government, although the government must continue with wise and constructive policies. You and I as individuals have to help make it happen. . . . We talk a lot about our religious and political heritage which we have inherited from our fore-bears. . . . This is how we honor that heritage—by creating a society that is not forever riven by racial antagonisms and division.

Here are some other things we can do that won't cost us anything and that each one of us will get satisfaction and joy from doing—things that will speed the day when we really do have one community and one state and one country and that will be true to our Christian faith: we can go out of our way to really get to know people of other races—that process enriches all of us; when people say or do things that are clearly racially biased whether from blacks or whites, we must speak out against them; we can be aware of our own racial blind spots and stereotypes; we can participate in community efforts to reduce racial prejudice; we can become informed about the concerns of people of other races; and we can make a personal commitment to the elimination of racism whenever and however it exists.

. . . We must remember that we are all in this together. Regardless of where we came from or what we look like or what our cultural and ethnic and religious differences are, we must remember that we were all made by the same God, the Lord and Father of us all.

—Speech, Grace Chapel Presbyterian Church, Madison, Mississippi, July 30, 2000.

The new realities require us to understand our mutual interdependence. Members of both races must reach out to each other in ways that transcend race. Poverty and ignorance know no skin color.

. . . Why can't we come together around a commitment to see that our common hopes and aspirations are realized by more of our fellow citizens? If we can unite to do that, I believe that the superficial differences of race—of what we look like—will begin to fade away as a basis for division.

. . . Sensitivity to the needs and feelings of our friends and neighbors, black and white, may not be unique to the South, but it is one of the region's most enduring qualities. It is a part of our heritage which must not be lost or diminished.

—Speech, Stennis Institute, Jackson, Mississippi, November 20, 2000.

How wide the gap still is between the races despite all the progress that we have made. And the gap exists not just between people in Mississippi and New York. . . . It exists in communities all over America, and eliminating that gap is the biggest challenge facing us in this country today.

It is one thing to make grandiose political pronouncements on that subject, but where the rubber hits the road is in the actual work that goes into building and maintaining a livable society and a unified country. That is going to require each one of us making a personal commitment to do what we can to eliminate racial prejudice and misunderstanding and mistrust. We must work at it together across racial lines to build communities that recognize our common humanity and our common destiny and each of us, black and white alike, must act to eliminate racism wherever it raises its ugly head.

—"Reflections on a Life of Public Service," speech, Millsaps College, Jackson, Mississippi, March 9, 2004.

The names James Chaney, Andrew Goodman, and Michael Schwerner are forever enshrined in that pantheon of heroes to whom all of us owe so much.

This event today is not only a celebration of the lives of these men but it is an affirming of the liberation which has come to us. And it is a liberation that has helped set us all free.

A few years ago when I served as governor we had a dinner at the Governor's Mansion in memory of the great civil rights leader, Medgar Evers. I said to his widow, Mrs. Myrlie Evers, on that occasion, "Mrs. Evers, we white folks owe you and your martyred husband as much as black folks do, for he freed us as well."

I would say the same thing about the supreme sacrifice made by these three young men. They were working to free all of us.

We were prisoners of a system that held us all down—that dictated what we felt free to say and whom we could associate with and how we lived our lives. We were all in bondage to an indefensible way of life that was at odds with the ideals that this country was founded on. This state has now started to come into its own as a result of that liberation.

. . . As far as we have come—as meaningful as the events of this day are—we have to recognize how far we still have to go to create a truly united country. There is still too much distrust and misunderstanding among the races; there are still too many situations where we are judged by what we look like rather than who we are; there is still too much stereotyping; there are still too many of us who are indifferent to the importance of the little gestures of kindness and courtesy and civility in our dealings with each other and especially across racial lines.

I have long believed that it is in places like Philadelphia and in Mississippi as a whole that we have a special opportunity and responsibility to demonstrate what a truly model multiracial society ought to be like. Because we have lived close together for so long—but too often in the past in a way that did not acknowledge our common humanity—now we can more easily realize the incredible potential that we have. But it will take a commitment that is expressed in actual deeds and not just in good intentions. It will mean reaching out beyond the old boundaries of race and class and seeking to achieve together what we cannot do separately. That will be how we most effectively justify the sacrifice of these young men whose memory we honor today. This is the torch that has been passed to us to carry and which we must pass on to another generation. It is a task that demands the best in all of us.

—Speech, delivered at the Chaney, Goodman, Schwerner Memorial, Philadelphia, Mississippi, June 20, 2004.

When all is said and done, though, the success or failure of integration in a given community is going to depend on the conviction of parents as to what will best serve their children. Admittedly the economic circumstances of some families will give them little choice. But for most the considerations will be based on a weighing of the factors of educational quality, safety, diversity, interpersonal relationships, and institutional policies and attitudes. The bottom line is that in most cases it will be the parents, and in some cases the children themselves, who will decide where they go to school. This is where black and white parents must come together to understand how they can support each other in maintaining strong public schools.

—"Before and after Brown in Mississippi," speech, George Washington University, July 1, 2004.

ON MARTIN LUTHER KING, JR.

It is a scene indelibly etched in my memory almost forty years later. I am still both haunted and inspired by that experience, My hometown of Grenada, Mississippi, like many other similar Deep South communities in the middle 1960s was faced with the desegregation of its public school. It had by August of 1966 come down to a final epic showdown between the forces of law and order and justice and dignity and those represented by the mindless advocates of fear and hate-driven violence who would destroy their community in order, in their own depraved thinking, to save it—save it from that ultimate calumny of having their schools open to all children.

The issue had been joined early that summer when the Southern Christian Leadership Conference established a presence in Grenada under the leadership of Dr. King and his colleagues, including Andrew Young. It was a bitter summer of almost nightly confrontation between scores of determined black followers of Dr. King and an angry bottle- and stick-throwing mob of Klansmen aided and abetted by the local sheriff who, if not an actual member of the Klan, was a strong Klan supporter. The threat of major violence was so real that the governor, for all of his earlier segregationist rhetoric, dispatched some fifty state highway patrolmen to Grenada to avert bloodshed. My hometown was a powder keg ready to explode.

Up until then as a state elected official (I was state treasurer at that time) I had publicly called for compliance with the law and deplored the kind of confrontation that had resulted in the tragedy at Ole Miss, but I had not done much more than that. Now the battle lines were closer to home, and even though I no longer lived in Grenada, I felt that I needed to do something.

On the Thursday before school was to begin for the fall term on the following Monday, I called some of my Grenada friends, including the Presbyterian minister, and asked if I could come up and meet with them. We met the next morning with my old college roommate, now a prominent business leader, and acknowledging that we were confronted with a major problem, we agreed to the concept of creating a biracial commission of local citizens to defuse the crisis.

In the meantime just as I was preparing to go back to Jackson, I got a frantic call from the Methodist minister who had been in our group.

"There is a rally going on at the Bell Flower Baptist Church," he told me. "Over three hundred black children are being organized to march together into the all-white crowd at the opening football game. The Klan is there waiting on them."

With no time to spare, my two minister friends and I drove to the church. We sought out the SCLC organizer and expressed our concern. He invited us into a hot and airless anteroom where local black leaders were gathered. I knew several of them, and I explained what we had been doing earlier in the day. We pleaded with them not to pursue the march.

"Give us until next week," we pleaded.

"But you have had all summer," they said.

We acknowledged the lateness of the hour, but we also were convinced that there would be a bloody riot if the march took place. For almost two hours we engaged in some of the most intense conversation in which I had ever been involved. Really I believe it was the first time that I had ever fully comprehended the intensity of the influence and spiritual force of Dr. King, and even though he was not personally present in that room I felt that he was there. He had infused into his followers the righteousness of the cause of justice to which they were all so totally committed. Our little group of white faces was no match for their passion. The only thing that we did succeed in that evening was to keep everybody talking until it was too late for the march.

I am convinced to this day that by doing so we averted what could have been and probably would have been a brutal and perhaps fatal confrontation in the dark shadows of that football stadium, where, as we later confirmed, many armed thugs of the Klan were awaiting the arrival of the marchers.

Those fears were further confirmed on Monday when school did finally open amid a scene of black children being beaten with baseball bats and bicycle chains and Klan hoodlums beating newspaper reporters into unconsciousness. We realized to our utter devastation our well-meaning efforts at reconciliation had been too little and too late.

Now forty years removed from that distant scene and despite all the progress that we have made since, I can say to you that what we are doing now is still too little and too late. If you don't believe that, you must have missed those tragic scenes that emerged from the horrors of Hurricane Katrina and that continue to haunt our memories of that nightmare. Just as we were beginning to feel pretty good about ourselves in this bustling, booming, affluent society where we have put behind us the bad old days of the segregated sixties, we have had thrust in our reluctant faces the reality of the chasm that still divides us in so many ways and in so many places in this country.

It may not be a divide marked as much by race per se as it was then, but it is nevertheless a huge and ever widening gap between those of us who have a lot and those who do not. It is a gap marked by those who have the advantage of a good education and those who do not. It is a gap marked by those who access to the levers of power and influence and those who do not. It is a gap marked by those who can get up every morning in a comfortable home on a safe street filled with hope and bright expectations and those who rise in misery every single day with little reason to believe that tomorrow will be any better than today.

As we look back we have to understand that this was the real mission that Dr. King was on—to eliminate or at least diminish all the gaps that keep us from being a united people. And it was not just for black people that he and others like him worked.

. . . This is really what our celebration for his birthday and his life must be about. It is one thing to proclaim his greatness and honor him by naming streets and buildings for him and by celebrating a national holiday in his memory. All of these things are appropriate and I applaud them. But I must tell you these are only symbols, tokens really, of what he stood for.

The only way an occasion like this one today is worth anything is that it be a part of the basis for each one of us to look in the mirror—to look inside ourselves—and ask that haunting question: What can I do? Not what can my neighbor do—not what can my club do—not what can my church do—to further the goals of brotherhood and sisterhood as personified and expressed in word and deed by Dr. King. It is what can I do.

That is not a question to be considered lightly and it cannot be answered easily. But I can tell you this, until and unless enough of us plain, ordinary citizens of this great country get together and start figuring out how we can play a more influential and meaningful role in setting some priorities that will provide a fuller and more mature understanding of how we should relate to each other, both in this country and with the people of the world, we are going to wind up in big trouble.

As I say this, I know your eyes glaze over. We have heard all this before, you are thinking. But that's a part of the problem. Too many of us have succumbed to those most insidious narcotics of all the drugs on the market. We have become overcome by those fatal, trance-inducing drugs of apathy, skepticism, and cynicism mixed in with a large dose of greed. How many times have I heard from some of my friends and in some of the college classes that I have presumed to teach from time to time the bored, plaintive protest, "What difference will I make? No, I don't vote, I don't count." Or more cynically, "What's in it for me?"

That response is a sulf-fulfilling prophecy. You didn't tell that to Dr. King. You didn't tell that to the marchers on the Pettus Bridge in Selma, Alabama. You didn't tell that to John Lewis—now Congressman John Lewis of Georgia—when he single-handedly defied one mob after the other. You didn't tell that to Medgar Evers in my state of Mississippi when at the risk of his life, he helped people register to vote.

. . . You may not get certified as martyrs or national heroes. But what you can do is help save our country and our world and restore our sense of purpose as inheritors of the legacy of Dr. King.

. . . In our political system we tend to ignore the most important office in that system. I had the privilege to serve as governor of my state one time. That is an important office. Certainly the office of president is. I do not mean to diminish the significance of those positions or any other public office when I tell you that the key to all political authority, though, is the office of private citizen. It is an office established by the U.S. Constitution. It does not have term limits. It is only from that office that all political authority comes. It is only from there that the policies of a people, for good or ill, are formulated and validated. And if the holders of that power do not take that responsibility seriously and do not exercise that power with integrity and intelligence and with concern for the public good, that system will fail.

If, for example, we turn our eyes away from the abuses of power by our elected or appointed agents; if we blithely cast our votes on the basis of the most superficial, or what is worse, prejudicial information; if we lazily refuse to do the reading and the serious inquiring and the discussing to be able to make our own informed decisions on public issues, then we are not worthy to call ourselves free citizens of this democracy.

This is the kind of enlightened citizen empowerment that Dr. King was talking about when he transformed a despairing and despondent black populace in Montgomery, Alabama, into a citizen force that ensured that not only was Rosa Parks able to sit anywhere she wanted to on a public bus but that ultimately every black citizen in America had access to all public accommodations.

It was the kind of response that caused an ignored and abused body of sanitation workers in Memphis to assert the legitimacy of their cause. It was the kind of tireless, unyielding, no turning back effort that I personally witnessed that night at the Bell Flower Baptist Church in my hometown.

Sometimes the price of such progress is very high as we all know from the assassination of Dr. King in Memphis on that fateful April day. But for the rest of us the price of apathy and inaction can be even higher. By being willing to go along to get along, by adopting an attitude that puts our own narrow selfish interests ahead of the community's interest, by failing to

challenge the religious and political charlatans who seek to
defame and discredit those working to achieve a more just
society, we dishonor the memory of Dr. King and diminish his
legacy and his work.

—"Remembering Dr. Martin Luther King, Jr.: His Unfinished Work," speech, Austin Theological
Seminary, Austin, Texas, February 2, 2006.

ON AN HUMANE AND
JUST SOCIETY

The fact that some things have changed does not mean that all
things have changed. What has not changed is the ideal that
is at the base of our human values and that forms the foundation of any humane and just society. That, simply put, is the
recognition of our obligation to each other. It is expressed in
the Biblical admonition that we are our brother's keeper. It
is expressed in the political ideal that we live under a social
contract that makes us responsible for more than just our own
well-being.

But there is great confusion these days about how this
is done without surrendering our individualism and self-
affirmation. The siren calls of a free-wheeling competitive
society entreat us to do our own thing. The TV ads say, "Just
do it." Indeed, the self-reliance about which Emerson so eloquently wrote has long been the inspiration for spectacular
achievement. But self-reliance and self-realization are one
thing. Self-indulgence and self-centeredness are another.

Mature people come to understand that they can develop
those qualities that make them creative and responsible individuals at the same time that they are able to honor values and
interests which lie beyond themselves. Only by establishing
the emotional and moral commitments to purposes beyond
one's self can we really live successfully in a free society. That

requires a discipline that is not easily taught. It requires an examination of what it is that gives meaning to our lives.

. . . A democratic society cannot leave . . . problems to be solved by blind chance or individual impulse. There must be a shared vision that recognizes our mutual interdependence, and advancing and clarifying that vision must be our common purpose. It is a vision that must be transmitted to our children, but it can be most effectively taught by our own individual performance and example.

For those of us who have been so greatly favored to have been the beneficiaries of a good education and the opportunity to enjoy social and financial success there is an obvious element of self-interest in all of this. Because we have so much we have more to lose if our society becomes unglued. But for most of us there surely must be a motivation that is beyond self-interest. That motivation in the final analysis will ultimately determine what kind of people we are and whether the ideals of truth and justice that we profess to believe in will be strengthened and preserved.

It will determine most importantly what kind of society we bequeath to our children and grandchildren. That is the only inheritance that really matters. It must be an inheritance that combines a commitment to social justice, environmental integrity, the education and development of all of our people and in an increasingly multicultural society the recognition and celebration of our common humanity.

—Speech, Davidson College, October 26, 1996.

ON PATRIOTISM

I hope that the events of September 2001 have helped us to develop a new perspective on just where we are. As a result of that tragic experience we have seen a surge of incredible patriotic fervor. Flags are waving all over the place, and that is a heartwarming response. Flags can be powerful symbols.

But let me remind you that patriotism is a lot more than the display of banners and symbols and the playing of martial music. It is more than feeling good about ourselves and our military response to the awful specter of terror. True and meaningful patriotism must involve doing those things that ensure that our country is going to be a better place for all of us in the future.

That patriotism must include an interest in the kind of educational system we have and our willingness to make the investments to pay for it. It must be denoted by our resolve to preserve and protect the natural bounty of rich land and clean air and clear streams that we inherited from an earlier generation. It must be reflected in our commitment to sustaining the kind of communities that people want to live in, where we don't have to exist in fear and ignorance of our neighbors and where our deeply held hopes and dreams can be fulfilled through hard work and where everybody is treated with dignity and respect.

It must in essence be based on the understanding that none of us is an island and that each one of us as citizens must be willing to put more in than we take out. The exclusive pursuit of self-interest is almost a sure-fire way to insure that our political and economic system will break down. Too many of us have been encouraged to adopt an attitude of getting while the getting is good. For some that has meant taking advantage of the perquisites of public office. For others in the corporate world of Enron and Worldcom it has meant claiming all the benefits and privileges of our economic system at the expense of innocent employees, stockholders, and consumers.

So it is time for all of us—and especially those of us who have been so greatly favored as to attain positions of leadership—to lead the return to a point of view that puts social and economic justice before private advantage—that puts community building at least on a par with personal empire building—and that understands that our own individual liberty is inextricably linked to our respect and concern for every other individual.

—Speech, Association of County Commissioners of Georgia and Municipal Association, Atlanta, Georgia, October 1, 2002.

Concern for and devotion to one's state and country I hope will never be considered out of date or old-fashioned, although we must all understand that these virtues mean a great deal more than just standing up when the flag goes by. They mean a willingness to make the sacrifice of time, of energies, of talents, and sometimes even life itself. In this connection I do not believe that history will ever record any greater examples of totally selfless devotion to duty than those related to the men like my own grandfather who wore the Confederate Gray. The fact that these men were subject to the ordinary wants and frailties of all of us—that they got tired and hungry and sick— makes all the more heroic their service and all the more meaningful one of the great stories that came out of the War.

This was a story of the desperate winter of 1863 in Virginia involving one of Jackson's famous foot-cavalrymen. The General, riding back along the column, came upon a soldier, too old and tired to fight but still slogging along. "Soldier," said the General, "do you think you can make it?" "Yes, General, I'll make it somehow," the old soldier replied. "But, General, I sure hopes to God I never loves another country."

The point was that this soldier did love his country and was desperately trying to serve it. This is the kind of dedication that is needed in the building of a state as well as in the fighting of a war.

—Speech, Hinds County Democratic Meeting, Mississippi, May 1964.

ON PRESERVATION AND CONSERVATION

We are seeing a greatly increased awareness of historic preservation—of the importance of saving the unique and irreplaceable reminders of our heritage. Local and regional planning agencies are now taking note of the desirability of maintaining the individuality of our communities and not letting them become plastic look-alikes. We cannot let all of our nineteenth- and early twentieth-century buildings, so many of which are physically sound and architecturally significant, be swallowed up by plastic pizza parlors and glittery motels.

—"The Ultimate Legacy," chapter in *Mississippi* 1990, published by University Press of Mississippi, 1979.

As the flow of people into the state continues . . . concerns with the preservation of a satisfactory natural environment will increase as well. There is now a growing recognition of the importance of setting aside wilderness areas for conservation and recreation. With most of our land still as fields and forests and possessed of an abundance of relatively clean lakes and rivers, Mississippians must be careful that we do not lose our birthright. In the preservation of this heritage must come a willingness to be selective in the location of major industrial sites and recognition that, in some instances, we must let public access to scenic areas take precedence over narrow economic interests. More wild streams and wilderness areas need to be identified and protected from misuse and exploitation. Mississippi probably should never attempt to compete with Florida or other states for hordes of tourists. We should show off to the best advantage the attractions that we have, and by doing so we shall undoubtedly have more and more visitors. But our principal concern from an esthetic and environmental position should be the protection of our natural beauty for the succeeding generations of people who will live here.

—"The Ultimate Legacy," chapter in *Mississippi* 1990, published by University Press of Mississippi, 1979.

Not only is it good sense to preserve these buildings as physical reminders of our culture but also it is in many instances plain good business to do so. The restoration of a well-built structure is in most instances more economical than building one from scratch. The result is both architectural beauty and sound business practice. Private citizens and public officials alike can render a great service . . . by being aware of buildings that ought to be preserved and supporting efforts to do so.

—Television commentary, WJTV, Jackson, Mississippi, 1985.

Where we human beings live in any considerable numbers, we inevitably create a lot of trash and garbage. The privilege of living in a country like ours carries with it the responsibility to take care of it, to protect it, to be proud of it. We don't show much love for or pride in our country when we clutter it up with all manner of debris. . . . The least we can do is to assume the responsibility for our own trash. That is a contribution that does not cost us a penny and does not involve much effort. The payoff is the preservation of a clean and beautiful land. What better bargain are we looking for?

—Television commentary, WJTV, Jackson, Mississippi, 1985.

Conservation has always come naturally to us Mississippians. We live close to the land, and we appreciate the wealth that it brings us in so many ways. Feelings born from generations of hunting, fishing and farming the land have produced in us a unique bond with our natural heritage, but I am concerned that we may be in danger of seeing that bond weaken, of forgetting our heritage and our collective ties to the land.

Not long ago I saw an editorial cartoon that emphasized that concern. The cartoon depicted Adam standing in Eden. He is surrounded by plants and animals. Above him is a cloud, and from the cloud the voice of God says, "And so I give the beasts of the earth, the fowl of the air, and every living thing unto your stewardship . . . to which Adam replies, "Please God, no more unfunded mandates."

Today our protection and stewardship for the world we live in is being reduced to an equation of cost effectiveness. People speak of infestations of red-cockaded woodpeckers as if they are rats that have invaded their homes. . . . And people refer to government ownership of land as if that government was some alien nation, and not a government elected by its citizens to take care of land owned by those same citizens.

—Speech, Mississippi Wildlife Federation, Jackson, Mississippi, February 21, 1996.

ON PUBLIC SERVICE

Even a textbook model for the organization of government will still fall short of achieving the desired results without the right kind of people. It is the performance and the attitude of the individual human beings which make the ultimate difference. That is why it is so important that we defend the concept that public service, despite all of its detractors, is a noble and worthy calling. Rather than running away from it, now is the time when participation in government service is more important than ever. Attracting the ablest people to public life remains essential to our future success.

—Speech, National Association of Secretaries of State, Portland, Maine, August 11, 1992.

EDUCATION

Kindergarten class, Tupelo, Mississippi, 1985. Authorization for kinder-
gartens, one of the principal programs of the Education Reform Act of
1982, began in school year 1985–86.

ON TEACHERS

Money alone may not guarantee better schools, but we are not going to get better schools and better teachers without it. The truth of the matter is that for a long time we have been getting some rare bargains in so many of our teachers.

—Television commentary, WJTV, Jackson, Mississippi, 1985.

We can come up with all kinds of high-sounding programs, but good education and good schools are still measured by the quality of the teaching and the leadership of the school administration. The most creative and carefully planned curriculum is no good unless it is administered and taught by caring, conscientious, and competent teachers. Attracting more of them into the classroom is the most effective school reform policy that I can think of.

—"The Politics of Educational Reform in a Diverse Society," speech, National Conference on Multicultural Education, New Orleans, Louisiana, August 1, 1992.

ON EDUCATION

If there is one priority that I would place above all the rest as the chief concern for Southern political leadership at the present time, it would be that of the maintenance of an effective educational system—not just the maintenance, but the improvement of such a system. This must mean a public educational system. . . . It is going to take the full resources of public support to assure educational opportunity for all who must have it if our region is to prosper.

We are now living in a world that will not let us forget that just because we come from a good family and joined the right clubs and lived in the right part of town our success is automatically assured. We are living in a world that is not interested in who we are or where we came from half as much as in what we can do. And for our state and our region we can compete in this world and in this nation only as we develop the processes of learning competent to meet the needs of a people that have their sights on the stars. This, in fact, is the area from which, in all probability, we shall soon see the vehicle emerge that will carry a man to the moon and back. The educational requirements of the predominantly agricultural society of a few years ago are no longer adequate to meet the stern requirements of today's age of space. They are not even adequate for the ever-growing demands of agriculture.

So the first and overriding call on the political leadership of the South in the years just ahead is the preservation of effective public education. We must not let anything interfere with the ability of the youth of this region to secure here in the region as good an education as is available anywhere in the country, and this opportunity must be available to all of the bright young men and women and not just to the chosen few. Only in this way can the South be true to its promise.

—"The Problems of Southern Politics," speech, All Saints' Junior College, Vicksburg, Mississippi, March 27, 1963.

Having begun my own formal education in a little one-room schoolhouse taught by my mother, I have always been impressed with two important facts about our system of education. The first fact is that as the need for more and better trained people increases, the greater the amount of our resources we must be willing to invest in our schools. And the second fact is that we must maintain as much local control and self-determination over our schools as we possibly can.

—Speech, Jaycees DSA Banquet, Vicksburg, Mississippi, January 18, 1965.

Too often we have regarded . . . elementary/secondary schools and universities/colleges . . . as somehow separate. Now we know better. We cannot have first-class higher education unless we have top quality education from kindergarten through high school. It is imperative that there be more . . . mutual involvement and cooperation . . . if we are to achieve maximum results from all of the elements of our educational system.

—Television commentary, WJTV, Jackson, Mississippi, 1985.

My experience in getting education reform moved to the top of the political agenda in Mississippi has convinced me that it must remain there if we are to get ahead. . . . The maximum development of our human resources in many different ways— adult literacy, preschool intervention programs for children at risk, drop-out prevention—remains the most critical challenge with which we are confronted.

—Speech, Leadership Florida, Orlando, Florida, March 24, 1990.

In order to keep up in this fast-moving global economy we are going to have to gear up our entire educational system for higher performance. That means higher performance not just for some folks but for everybody.

   That is not going to be easy. It is not going to be easy—not because we lack the resources or the understanding of what ought to be done. It is not going to be easy because not enough of us in this country have come to grips with the realities of what we are confronted with. That is particularly true in this section of the country where we do not have a well-defined tradition of putting education at the top of our personal and political agendas.

. . . There are two fundamental requirements that have to be met if we are going to reconcile the ever-contesting demands of access and quality. First, we must establish clear and acceptable standards arranged in a proper sequence all the way from kindergarten through higher education. Secondly, we must prepare students to meet those standards so that they may gain access not just to a diploma but to progressively higher levels of education. In the language of the marketplace it is a matter of leveling up instead of leveling down. This is a difficult process. It is easier to do it in reverse, especially when there is a pay-off for increased enrollments. Maybe at one time there was a semblance of equity in doing it that way. Now we are beginning to understand that it is not fair to anybody, particularly to those from minority and disadvantaged backgrounds, to award diplomas, whether from high school or college that are not valid certificates of academic achievement. And it is a denial of equal opportunity to have a student graduate from an institution that is stamped in the public mind as having an inferior program.

One of the basic reforms involves a defining of what constitutes college-level work. Higher education has frequently been slow to acknowledge that too much of what is credited as college work is not. Standards must be adopted that recognize basic academic skills, such as reading and writing. It is not fair to the students nor to the faculty who struggle to teach them when those students obviously cannot compete at the college level.

. . . Formal, stereotyped education alone . . . is not enough. There must also be communicated a vision of what can be accomplished. We cannot stay in the same comfortable ruts doing things the same way. The institutions and communities and individuals that will prevail and prosper will be those who seek challenge and change and welcome them as avenues to a better and more meaningful existence.

—"Issues and an Agenda for Education in the 1990s," speech, Southern Association of Colleges and Schools Meeting, Atlanta, Georgia, April 2, 1990.

Education must also be the means of transmitting a set of values based on a belief in the worth and dignity of every human being. It must teach us how to make hard decisions, to take chances and defy risks; to stretch ourselves to limits that may exceed our grasp, but that all add to the ultimate strength and resiliency of the human spirit. It must teach us how to get along in harmony with ourselves and with each other and especially with those who are different from us. How to govern and how to serve, how to be conservative in the assertion of our rights and liberal in the extension of those rights to others. It must teach us in essence how to live, with all the confidence and self-assurance and compassion that are the true measures of educated men and women.

—Speech, University of Montevallo, April 11, 1991.

When we speak of educational reform, there is a tendency to look at it as a process either that we have just completed or just discovered. We point with pride to what has been accomplished, while on the other hand we view with alarm the unfinished business that still confronts us.

The fact of the matter is that our educational systems, like most other human enterprises, represent a constantly evolving process which is affected by the various social and economic developments that are an ever-changing part of our existence. It is when we become oblivious to these influences or deny their existence that we create trouble for ourselves and limit our ability to construct the kind of productive and competitive society that we ought to have.

. . . This then should be the first objective of any reform effort, past or present—to create a system where nobody gets left out. That was the driving force behind my efforts as governor of Mississippi in the early eighties to improve our schools in a way that would afford every single child a globally competitive education. That remains the still elusive objective of present and future efforts at reform.

The politics of reform was then, as it is now, to compel enough people to understand the vital importance of having a universally trained citizenry and to present a sufficiently credible plan that makes them willing to support it with their resources and their individual efforts.

. . . Our undeveloped human capital remains our greatest barrier to economic growth and prosperity in this country. The plain fact is that as long as we have as many undereducated people as we have, we are going to lag in the race for international leadership. Education is the only thing that will unlock the door to economic progress.

. . . The politics of reform now must involve making more people aware of what is happening in our work force. This country now must look for its needed strength in its newly recognized diversity.

. . . The next major initiative must recognize that it is not enough to concentrate on the school systems alone. We cannot impose a burden on the schools that they are unable to bear. We must find a means to impact in an effective way the conditions that cause children to enter school too impaired to compete. This is obviously going to be an expensive and complex process, but unless we attack the root problems of poverty and health care—of drug abuse and teenage pregnancy—of social alienation and self-destructive life styles, we are not going to improve the products of our educational system.

. . . The politics of it is, though, that out of self-interest people must understand that we cannot afford to write off 25 percent of our population as permanently nonproductive. It is not just a matter of justice and equity. Our future as a nation depends on our ability to educate and make productive all of our people.

. . . If continuing progress is going to be made in improving the quality of our schools and ensuring equity for everyone in our uniquely diverse society, it will be done, as meaningful reform has always been accomplished, by creating a shared vision of what we want our communities and our country to be. We must help more of our fellow citizens to understand that we cannot live in little enclaves isolated and remote from the needs and problems of the larger community.

—"The Politics of Educational Reform in a Diverse Society," speech, National Conference on Multicultural Education, New Orleans, Louisiana, August 1, 1992.

Poorly educated people translate into poor people. Education is the one thing that will break the cycle of poverty. It is the only thing that will unlock the door of economic opportunity.

—Speech, Southern Growth Policies Board, Atlanta, Georgia, December 10, 1992.

There are still too many schools which are not producing satisfactory results. When we permit this to happen, we are killing the dream that so many people have had of a society where nobody gets left out. Children of whatever race get left out when they are obliged to attend schools that do not provide them with a competitive education.

. . . There must first of all be an understanding that we shall succeed only by making our schools places where students not only learn how to make a living but also how to live together. This is more important now than it was forty years ago, because our world has gotten smaller and our nation has grown more racially diverse. . . . America is the most diverse democracy in the world, but it must also be a democracy united by shared values. Vital to this process is an educational system that has student bodies that are truly representative of that diversity. Only in that way will our children have an opportunity for the experiences that will prepare them to live confidently in this complex and economically demanding world.

. . . It is not enough that we have diversity as a single goal. That would be a hollow victory . . . unless those schools are equipped to produce the kind of academically prepared graduates who can compete in the job market. This is an absolutely critical factor in fashioning educational policy. We owe it to all those who fought so long for access to make certain that we do not forsake quality.

. . . We all know the vast unevenness in the effectiveness of our schools. Too often social and economic factors decide how good or how poor schools are, and too often the poorest areas, which frequently means the minority areas, are the communities with the poorest schools. This also means that these are the schools that are the most difficult to integrate.

. . . Active, interested parental support of their children's school activities is an almost essential element. When that is lacking, and there are obvious reasons especially for poor, single, working mothers for it to be lacking, more often than not the children pay a price. As hard as they try, the schools cannot make up for parental guidance and support. This opens up an entire separate area of concern, and that is the social and economic conditions that limit children's opportunity to achieve. Physical access to good schools unaccompanied by an increased effort at improving the family circumstances in which so many children live will not produce One America.

. . . We must get the message out to every household and especially every poor household that the only road out of poverty runs by the schoolhouse. Discrimination in this country is not confined to the fault lines of race. The line that separates the well-educated from the poorly educated is one of the harshest dividers of all.

—"The Desegregation of America's Schools: A Dream Unrealized," speech, Little Rock, Arkansas, September 26, 1997.

Failure to educate adequately so many of our people is at the heart of our problem. In the past it was the result of a lack of priority and thus a lack of investment in education. Now it is partially at least the result of limited expectations and lowered standards. Too many children, especially blacks and poor whites, find themselves in schools or classes which do not provide them with the skills they need to compete at the college level or in the workplace. While advances are being made, there are still too many schools that do not offer the rigorous curriculum necessary for future academic success. . . . Students cannot learn what they are not taught. Students cannot compete at the college level if they are shortchanged at the elementary and secondary level.

—"From the Ivory Tower to the Mean Streets: Higher Education's Role in Community Building," speech, Tufts University, June 12, 1998.

ON *BROWN V. THE BOARD OF EDUCATION*, 1954

For a few weeks there was an ominous quiet as if no one really could fathom what the appropriate reaction should be. There was no word from the White House in support of the decision. That was unfortunate, given the fact that President Eisenhower was enjoying enormous popularity in the South at that time. Many of the young Southern business and political leaders had served under him during World War II. He had a credibility that would have provided a large umbrella against the gathering storm.

The first flashes of lightning appeared in the Delta sky in July. Mid-summer in that vast sweep of flat, lush greenness brings a tropic temperature that at two o'clock in the afternoon creates a shimmering ocean of heat rays rippling as far as the eye can see across the unending fields. The stifling climate was an ever-present irritant that, in the days before air-conditioning, had the capacity to drive otherwise mature and reasonable individuals into a kind of torpor that created morbid visions of tragedy and disaster. In the heat of the Mississippi Delta the old ghosts of the Civil War could easily be resurrected. In their reincarnation the new ghosts took the form of the black field hands and their nameless counterparts slumped in the steamy shade of a thousand wretched, stinking back alleys in the little Delta towns. The demonic fears had always been there. Now the *Brown* decision gave them a new and urgent reality.

The first meeting to resist the decision took place in Indianola in the heart of the Delta. Some of the area's leading white citizens were there. A few days later a larger gathering was called for Greenwood. As the state representative I was invited to go by some of my Grenada County constituents who were understandably concerned about the decision. The auditorium of the city hall was packed. There were lurid descriptions by some of the planters of subversive black activity, particularly as it related to alleged plots to register to vote. Several suggested as a first step the abolition of the public schools. The consensus was that the people had to be made to understand that if they just stuck together, they could find ways to circumvent by state action the decisions of the federal courts. I stood up and cautiously expressed doubt that it was that simple. I recalled that the Supreme Court had said that it was impermissible to try to accomplish indirectly what had been forbidden to be done directly. That was obviously not what most of the audience had come there to hear. One of the area's most respected lawyers told me privately after the meeting that he thought I was right, but he was the only one. It was increasingly apparent that we were in for several long, hot summers.

I did not realize it at the time, but I was witnessing the birth of the White Citizens Council. Before the year was over, it would be organized in a number of counties, and would begin to be a major political force in the state. I respectfully declined overtures to join.

—Unpublished personal memoirs.

He was maybe my best friend. Perhaps more like a big brother. Two years older than I, he was bigger, stronger, more athletic. His real name was Elmo, but everyone called him Cricket. Growing up together on my father's farm, we did all the things that teenage boys in those circumstances did. We fished and swam and played together. We visited in each other's homes. We spent numberless summer days together, but when school started each fall, Cricket and I saw less and less of each other.

For, you see, Cricket was black, and we couldn't go to school together. While I would board a comfortable bus for the ten-mile ride into the county seat to an impressive twelve-grade school which ran for nine months each year, Cricket and his black friends were obliged to walk some two miles to a little one-room, six-grade school taught by one teacher that ran for five months. My bus would pass them on cold, rainy winter mornings, and I would wave to Cricket. It was a lot better to be a white boy I told myself. I went on to finish high school and then to get a law degree from Ole Miss. Cricket never got past the sixth grade.

That's how it was in the Deep South when I was growing up in Mississippi in the 1930s. Education, we were told, was not meant for everybody. We had an economic system that was based on maintaining a large supply of unskilled labor. Too much formal schooling would ruin a good field hand they said. And not all of those field hands were black.

As a white boy in the South in those depression years, I was a product of a social and economic arrangement that imposed a strict system of segregation between the races in schools. . . . Despite the clear language of the Fourteenth Amendment, the

Supreme Court acquiesced in this result by establishing the doctrine of "separate but equal" in the *Plessy v. Ferguson* decision in 1896.

That doctrine, which was embraced by most white Southerners, neglected in actual practice to give much recognition to the word "equal." The result was that in the field of education the grossest kind of disparity existed between white schools and black schools. This was the situation when my friend, Cricket, and I were going to school.

. . . But now fifty years after *Brown* we still have not overcome the difficulties of the past. Across the South there remain too many underfunded and ill-managed schools, especially in the poor areas. There is still too much white flight. There are still too many schools which are not producing satisfactory results. When we permit this to happen, we are killing the dream that so many people have had of a society where nobody gets left out. Children of whatever race get left out when they are obliged to attend schools that do not provide them with a competitive education. That remains a major challenge that still faces us today, and until and unless we solve it we shall fall short as a competitive nation in the future.

—"Before and after *Brown* in Mississippi," speech, George Washington University, July 1, 2004.

ON UNIVERSITIES

It is in the final analysis a place where values are developed out of the testing that comes in the free exchange of ideas—many of them wrought out of heartache and hardship—out of the pain of defeat as well as the exhilaration of victory—out of the sacrifice that comes with the bad times as well as the bounty that comes with the good.

—Remarks, University of Mississippi Hall of Fame, October 27, 1989.

Most of us outside the formal structure of higher education have tended to take it for granted. We get most concerned when our alma mater does not win as many football games as we thought it should. But for the most part, we do not concern ourselves with the more vital aspects of higher education.

We are therefore surprised when someone asks, "Is higher education at risk?" The answer should be obvious. Of course, it is. Higher education has always been at risk. It has been at risk down through the centuries at the hands of those who have felt threatened by its persistent pursuit of truth and by its commitment to constructive change. It has been at risk to those who would profane its institutions with appeals based on prejudice and demagoguery. It has been at risk to those who would intimidate its teachers and confuse its patrons.

All of us . . . can recall out of our personal experiences or out of the lessons of recent history those too frequent occasions in the past when great educational institutions and great educators were subjected to humiliation and indignities at the hands of the blindly ignorant and the fanatically obsessed. What price we have paid here in our own region for the political intrusions in the years gone by! And while we have come a long way, we can never be certain that these intrusions will not happen again.

There was another time not so long ago when higher education was put at risk by those who naively advocated a policy of total access, where academic requirements were dismissed as being somehow irrelevant, where truth was what anyone, however undiscriminating, might want to make it. . . . We found that higher education could be done in by policies that let everybody in as well as by policies that tried to keep some people out.

Higher education has been put at risk by those who would use it to promote an insular or self-serving social or political point of view and where indoctrination has supplanted learning. It has been effectively put at risk by all manner of charlatans and scoundrels and imposters parading under the robes of supposedly noble causes but which in the end have proven to be self-serving and self-defeating.

Now we are in a new era when the risks are different, but the risks we face now may be the hardest to overcome. What I am talking about are the difficulties which higher education is facing in a time of financial retrenchment. The irony is that this lessening of support is coming at the very time when our institutions are being called on to do more and more.

In the first place, they are called on to educate an increasing percentage of our population. Our society is finally recognizing that we can compete in the global economy only as we educate all of our people. We understand that we can no longer afford to waste any of our human resources. This means that we have to provide education beyond the secondary level for more students. But it also means that we are imposing huge additional burdens on our institutions of higher learning to prepare more people for productive careers. Many of those entrants are coming ill prepared and yet we cannot afford to turn them away. Thus we add the very high expense of providing remedial education to an already overstretched budget.

In addition, we are turning increasingly to the colleges and universities for economic development strategies that will enable us to take fuller advantage of our opportunities. . . . This is a role that was largely unheard of just a few years ago. Now it is an indispensable but very expensive mission that higher education is committed to.

Higher education is the segment of our society where answers to some of our most intractable social and economic problems are being looked for. It is in the laboratories and libraries of the universities that solutions for everything from AIDS to political apathy are being studied and sought out. Projects and policies that affect how we live our lives and, indeed, our very life itself, are more and more having their origins on university campuses.

The point is that whether we know it or not the institutions of higher learning—public and private—are playing an absolutely indispensable role in charting a course for the future and providing not only an education for our children but a better life for us all. These results do not, however, come easily or without cost. They come only as we are willing to make the proper investments in our systems of higher learning.

This is more important for those of us who live in this region than for those who live elsewhere. This is because we are still catching up to the rest of the country. In the words of the 1986 report of the Commission on the Future of the South, "We are halfway home and a long way to go."

. . . Naturally suspicious of the intellectual and the academic, the average citizen of this region has to be made more comfortable with what the intellectual is capable of doing to make the lives of all of us better.

. . . There must be an understanding that there are no easy shortcuts or quick fixes as much as some would have us believe otherwise. We have to understand that quality in higher education is related directly to a demanding and challenging curriculum, to the devotion of faculties to teaching, and to the strengthening of the relationship between teachers and students. There is much that remains to be done to reach this level. It cannot be done without adequate understanding by an informed citizenry that also includes the policymakers— governors, legislators, and board members—of the difficult decisions that have to be made. No longer can we afford the luxury of the easy accommodations that have so often existed in the past. We can't afford cheap diplomas and admission on demand. But we also can't afford to leave too many students behind on the ash heap of indifference and neglect.

—"Who Benefits? Who Pays?" speech, Governor's Conference on Higher Education, Montgomery, Alabama, January 30, 1992.

One of the little noticed but significant developments in American higher education in the last ten to fifteen years has been an increasing acceptance of its role in the transformation of the larger community of which it is such a vital part. This is a role that is going to be increasingly important as we search for effective ways to sustain a stable society in the face of growing racial and cultural diversity.

. . . In the last decade . . . there has been tremendously increased involvement of colleges and universities . . . more and more hands-on efforts . . . to aid private business and local government. This has resulted in the creation of billions of dollars of new wealth that has helped to stimulate and sustain the economic boom of the 1990s.

But now there is a larger responsibility. It is the specific task of community building not just in a physical or economic sense but in a civic and social sense. This is an area that too many institutions of learning have neglected. It is now where very critical needs exist.

The role of higher education in community building consists of two basic functions. The first and most obvious is to create an understanding on the part of individual students of the importance of their role as responsible and compassionate citizens in a democratic society. The other is the responsibility of the university to use its resources to help build the civic relationships that make for strong communities.

. . . What should a responsible citizen be able to do and how does the undergraduate experience develop those abilities? We are not talking here about restructuring the curriculum or instilling political partisanship or threatening the liberal arts or limiting the prerogatives of the faculty. We are simply talking about shoring up the foundations of our democratic system by developing a sensitivity as to the academy's role in it.

. . . Colleges and universities must create the experiences required to develop civic competencies. If civic education is to be real, it must extend beyond the civics classroom and encompass all disciplines. It must help to instill the element of civic courage that enables people to look beyond the narrow, self-serving interests of their private lives and confront and embrace the opportunities to build a free and more just society. These opportunities abound today as never before.

. . . It is on the college campuses of America that the theory and the practice of civic learning can best be carried out. . . . For over three hundred years higher education has been a vehicle by which the next generation of citizen leaders have learned about their public responsibilities.

. . . The colleges and universities who are committed to access as well as quality must get more involved in the sources of supply of their students. Higher education has an increased responsibility to help provide the know-how, the resources, and the leadership to make elementary and secondary schools, and especially the poorer schools, more effective. It is not fair to anybody, and especially to the students involved, for high schools to turn out graduates who cannot compete in college or the workplace.

. . . It is on university and college campuses that young people can have the best opportunity they will ever have for the life experiences and the relationships that will prepare them to live successfully in a complex and demanding world.

. . . The task of building the kind of communities that will serve our nation in the future and unify us as a people can only be carried out by an increased commitment on the part of the nation's ultimate best hope against ignorance and bigotry—our universities and colleges.

—"From the Ivory Tower to the Mean Streets: Higher Education's Role in Community Building," speech, Tufts University, June 12, 1998.

In the final analysis what we must be ultimately measured by goes to the very reason for the existence of a university. The element that I believe separates the really great universities from the others is the degree to which a university is committed to the defense of its institutional independence and integrity and in its commitment to the pursuit of honest intellectual inquiry. This can be an incredibly harsh and demanding measure of judgement. It goes without saying that it frequently requires great courage.

I am not so naive as to fail to recognize the complex political realities that confront any public institution. We are oblivious to those realities at our peril. The pressure of political and public opinion can under certain conditions be overwhelming.

. . . But I do insist that we cannot undertake the task of meeting that final test of a great university except by making a commitment so clear that no one can doubt our resolve that this . . . will be a place where the honest search for truth will always be protected and preserved.

It is my observation that the schools which have in the past laid out legitimate claim to being great universities have been those institutions where this kind of integrity has existed. Some of them achieved greatness as a result of defending this concept.

. . . It is easy to be supportive when everyone is smiling and the band is playing and the teams are winning and the choices are simple. But sooner or later there comes a time when a controversial speaker may come to town or a professor may express an unpopular opinion or a group of students may develop some unorthodox political ideas. That is when mature unwavering support . . . must be expressed. There have been too many times in the past when we did not stand up.

. . . The test of a great university is what impact its influence has on shaping the thoughts and goals and values of the state and region of which it is a part. This mission goes beyond turning out professionally skilled graduates capable of competing in the world marketplace. . . . What we must also do is create . . .

an atmosphere that puts a unique stamp on the students who come . . . by vesting them with the vision and the civic courage to confront and deal with difficult public issues and to lead in the creation of a sense of responsibility for molding and shaping public opinion in an unselfish and open and visionary way. It is a sad commentary on our society when the inane and preposterous opinions expressed on talk radio and some TV shows carry more weight with many people than the thoughtful voices of reason. . . . [Universities] must be dedicated and looked to to produce those voices of reason.

—Found in writings for a possible commencement address in 2003.

Universities must teach that in this socially and economically diverse nation there must always be room for honest dissent and reasonable compromise. Our students must be helped to understand that our future will be diminished if we let bitterness and rancor and anger and greed control the political agenda.

—"Cultural Change, Community Building, and Civic Responsibility," speech, SACS—Commission on Colleges, Atlanta, Georgia, December 7, 2004.

ON THE UNIVERSITY OF MISSISSIPPI MEDICAL CENTER

I can remember well when we did not have a four-year medical school in our state. There was only a small two-year school housed in one small building on the Ole Miss campus at Oxford. While that facility was well regarded, all of its graduates were obliged to transfer to other schools out of state for their subsequent training. Not only were many of our people deprived of an opportunity to become physicians and health care professionals, but it was a costly brain drain for our state. Almost one-half of those who went away to school never came back to Mississippi. It was obvious that something had to be done if our state was to fulfill its obligation to its people.

It was my good fortune to have had a ringside seat at the series of events in 1950, when after years of talking about it, the legislature finally voted to establish a four-year school. There were eleven of us who were enrolled in Law School at Ole Miss who had just been elected to the House of Representatives. Authorizing the funding of a four-year medical school was high on our list of priorities. Most of us had included it in our campaign promises. We came to Jackson in January 1948 for our first session with high expectations.

Then we came face to face with the old arguments that had held us back before. "We can't afford it," the conservative old guard told us. "It may mean we will have to raise taxes," they said. And so nothing happened for another two years. But finally it did happen. I shall never forget that day in March 1950 when it did. It was a lengthy and heated debate.

. . . The clinching and climatic speech came from Representative Blaine Eaton of rural Smith County. His words I believe are worth repeating as we remind ourselves of our continuing responsibilities to support this school and, for that matter, our entire educational system today. In answer to those who said we couldn't afford a four-year medical school and with reference to the ever-present issue of race which was used by some of the opponents, this is what Blaine Eaton said on that day in March fifty-five years ago:

"I don't care if it costs five million dollars to save the life of one child. Some people can't help it because their papa or mama didn't inherit a plantation to go to college. I don't care whether they are white or black. They are just as much citizens as you are. You can't put a price on their heads. If you do, you have forgotten all the good that was born in you."

That speech, as much as any one thing, helped to pass the bill. . . . All of us present-day Mississippians and especially

those of you in this graduating class are the beneficiaries of
the rewards of that long-ago act by a group of courageous and
visionary citizens and legislators who came together to create
this institution. . . . I emphasize it primarily to point out the
obligation which each one of us has to reflect in our lives, in
Blaine Eaton's words, that "good that was born in (us)."

Nowhere, it seems to me, is that responsibility more relevant than in the profession of medicine and health care. You
could not have been called to this noble work of healing the
sick and caring for the afflicted and saving lives if there did not
exist deep within you an abiding commitment to service to
others that transcends all other considerations.

That must mean that, more than for most other people,
you recognize the validity of a social contract that binds us
to each other and that commands us to help and support each
other. The demands of that contract are driven by the idealism
on which this nation was built. It is expressed in that most
fundamental of our political documents, the Declaration of
Independence, when our forebears pledged to each other "their
lives, their fortunes and their sacred honor."

As you accept these diplomas certifying your eligibility . . . to
be members of this great health care profession in all of its many
vital facets, I hope that you will understand that at the same time
you are adding to your obligations under that social contract.
With every enhanced privilege that comes to us there also come
expanded responsibilities to those with whom we live.

We live in a time of great challenge and great peril, but we
also live in a time of unparalleled affluence and opportunity.
The advances in health care and medical research boggle the
mind. The promise of future breakthroughs is more amazing still.

But to achieve the ultimate results that we are capable of
will require our most careful setting of priorities. It is going
to be based on what as a society we consider most important.

It is going to depend on how we allocate our resources in this incredibly wealthy nation not on what is most important to us as individuals but on what is most important to our society and to the well being of those who will come after us. As the grandfather of five . . . I want to be assured that they will be able to inherit a state and country that will provide them the stability and quality of life that is at least as good as that which you and I now enjoy.

That means that we have to be willing to invest more of our finite resources in those investments where the pay-off is the greatest—in institutions of higher learning . . . and in education in general, in scientific research and in the conquest of disease, in protecting and preserving our natural resources, in strengthening and building institutions for peace and understanding, and in the elimination of violence. These are real tasks that all of us must be involved in pursuing. This obligation falls especially heavily on folks like you and me, because we have been so greatly blessed. I know that you will not fail.

Now let me close these remarks by telling you about a friend of mine. It was in the desperate fall of 1943 when this country was battling for its existence in World War II. I was a private in an infantry company undergoing basic training. My bunkmate was a young man about my own age named Regis Wancheck. He was the son of a Polish coal miner from Western Pennsylvania. I was a country boy from Mississippi.

In the course of training together we became the closest of friends in spite of our diverse backgrounds. His father had developed black lung disease in the mines. My friend's ambition he told me was to go to medical school after the war and minister to the miners like his father.

After our training ended, he went one way, and I went another, but we continued to exchange letters. In his last letter he wrote of being involved in the brutal fighting in the Philippines and of how he had won a battlefield commission.

I responded, but my letter was returned. It was marked, "Undeliverable—Killed in Action."

A short time afterwards I found myself in an infantry division in Manila—after the fighting had ended. I went to the newly created military cemetery there and amid the mounds of raw earth marking the graves of several thousand American soldiers who had been killed in the liberation of the Philippines I found a white wooden cross bearing the name Regis Wancheck. I knelt beside the grave of my fallen friend and said a prayer. I could only think what a great physician he would have been.

Regis did not get to go to medical school, but by his sacrifice he helped make it possible for you to go and for all of us to enjoy the privileges that have come our way. He was a silent party to that contract that pledged his life and his sacred honor to the fulfillment of his obligation as an American citizen.

. . . I hope that you will always remember your debt to so many who have enabled you to be here—to your parents, your teachers, your friends and neighbors and to the likes of Blaine Eaton and Regis Wancheck.

—"Paying Off the Debt," speech, fiftieth-anniversary commencement of the four-year University of Mississippi School of Medicine, Jackson, Mississippi, May 27, 2005.

LITERATURE
AND HISTORY

The governor welcomes to the Governor's Mansion four of Mississippi's most acclaimed writers, September 1, 1982. From left—Walker Percy, Margaret Walker Alexander, Governor Winter, Eudora Welty, and Shelby Foote.

ON MISSISSIPPI WRITERS

One of the questions that as governor I was asked over and over
by people in other parts of the country and, for that matter, in
other countries was, "What is Mississippi really like?" I found
in my conversations that our state has a certain mystique that
seems to set it apart even from the rest of the South. And for
the most part it is no longer a negative perception. It is rather
an innocent curiosity about a state that in spite of or maybe
because of hardship and adversity has maintained a sense of
place and family ties and a concern for where we have come
from. This mystique has I think really been inspired and given
substance by that remarkable group of writers who have come
out of Mississippi. Someone has said that for a state where a lot
of folks can't read, we certainly can write. We have to acknowledge that none of us nor our state will ever be the same because
of what they wrote, for what they wrote was about us and
about the triumphs of the human spirit.

—Television commentary, WJTV, Jackson, Mississippi, 1985.

It was the literature of Faulkner, of . . . Welty . . . writing stories about people and places they knew, their own postage
stamp, as Faulkner once said. It is this kind of storytelling that
is the basic element of great literature. And because it consists
of exploring the lives of people, some ordinary lives but others
complex and different, that we find in them mirrors of our own
lives as well as fantasies of lives we could never know, but out

of that reading we come to understand better who we are
and how we relate to each other. There is a magic about this
that has the power to transform people from spiritless apathy
to an awareness of their full potential for creative thought
and work.

—"Literature and the People," speech, Conference for the Book, University of Mississippi,
April 12, 1996.

For those of us who, like Willie, were, to use his word, inef-
fably affected by growing up in a Mississippi of myths and leg-
ends, of fantasy about what never was and hope for what might
never be, of insufferable baseness and incredible goodness, he
was the one who perhaps more than anybody else of our generation caused us to look within ourselves and discover there
the joy and inspiration to sustain us through the good times
and the bad.

I know that was true for me back in the late 1960s when
I first heard about Willie Morris and when I was looking desperately for some voices that would speak of what I thought
the South was really about—of civility and courtesy and kindness and tolerance—not of rage and hate and bitterness and
bigotry. I found in his writings the special insight of one whose
affection for his home state was not only undiminished but
reenforced by his recognition of our weaknesses as well as
our strengths and especially of our need to reach out to more,
indeed to all, of our neighbors, and to erase the barriers that
separated us from one another.

There was no meanness and there was no pretense in Willie
Morris. While not a publicly religious man, his life personified
what true religion is all about. He found it not in the usual
places but in the places where his friends were—in his words
"at the ball games and bus stations and courthouses and the
bargain-rate beauty parlors and the little churches and the road-
houses and the joints near closing time."

Willie found goodness and kindness in people wherever he met them. As an old Mississippi farmer said, "He didn't cull nobody."

—"Remembering Willie Morris," eulogy, Yazoo City, Mississippi, August 5, 1999.

Eudora Welty often wrote, as she did most memorably in *The Optimist's Daughter*, of the magic of coming together— "confluence" was the word which she liked to use—of people and places and events and time converging as did the great rivers at Cairo, Illinois, beneath the railroad tracks that carried Laurel Hand home to Mount Salus.

Eudora wrote that "the greatest confluence of all is that which makes up the human memory." "My own memory," she writes, "is the treasure most dearly regarded by me, in my life and in my work as a writer."

And that is the treasure that each of us must surely cherish in our coming together today not to mourn the passing of this great lady but to share and celebrate the enchanting memories of her life with us—not to make too much fuss over her incomparable literary achievements but to recall her as our unpretentious and self-effacing friend—not to eulogize her for her greatness as a writer but to acclaim her for the qualities that made her perhaps the most gracious and generous human being that any of us ever knew.

And Eudora will continue to live in our memories—in a thousand stories both of her telling and of our own about her— in her unfailing faith in the basic goodness of the everyday people that she knew and loved and in her disdain for the arrogant and the pompous—in her concern for and encouragement of young aspiring writers—in her remembered acts of incredible generosity . . . and her almost unnoticed gestures of courtesy and kindness at places like the neighborhood grocery store—in short in making her community and her world the better for her having passed this way.

. . . She has the rare capacity to define with eloquence and sensitivity those elements of the human spirit that link us all together in some wonderful and mysterious way, whether we be from Paris or Jackson or Tishomingo County.

. . . Because of who she was, and what she has written, many of the barriers that have separated us have been lifted, and she has caused us to understand one of the fundamental truths of our existence—that we cannot be indifferent to each other.

—Eulogy, Jackson, Mississippi, July 26, 2001.

ON THE BANNING OF BOOKS

In our increasing absorption with the attainment of limited, although in many cases admittedly worthy, goals—economic security, technical proficiency, political preferment, social acceptance—many of us I fear have become guilty of not using all of the knowledge and understanding and common sense that we possess. How many of us in how many varied circumstances have been parties to acquiescing in and tacitly accepting—even agreeing with—contentions and positions that we know to be false and untenable? We have let ourselves swallow (sometime gagging a little) in the interest of "getting along" a good many proposals and suggestions made in the name of patriotism or freedom or some other worthy cause that really have had nothing to do with either patriotism or freedom and in fact have been inconsistent with the real meaning of both. I think that the time has come to put a halt to this compromising of our intellectual integrity and to face up to some of the responsibilities which you and I have to call the hands of those who would confuse our children.

My appeal to you . . . is to use your identity as keepers of the brains—the schools being the great guardians of man's accumulated wisdom and the interpreters and perpetuators of that wisdom—to help keep the records straight. There are enough false statements being palmed off as gospel truth on the people these days to make most self-respecting citizens throw up their hands in disgust and despair. . . . We have recently seen the spectacle of self-styled experts on textbooks going around over our state peddling the myth that patriotic educators who have devoted their lives to the education of our children have somehow become either subversives or dupes. School teachers and administrators of proven ability and integrity have had their methods, their motives, and their morality assailed from behind a smokescreen of holier-than-thou positions.

. . . We have gotten along pretty well in this state for a long time in rearing our children in accordance with the highest traditions of the American system. Love of country has always been a foremost concern of the people of our state, but it has been a love of country free of suspicion and fear. It has been a love of country based on the idea that truth and our national destiny were somehow intertwined together, and that in the search for truth we would eventually realize our full destiny as a people.

It has been a love of country based on a respect for honest differences of opinion and on understanding that the rights of every individual citizen to hold to his own convictions and to express those convictions were the highest of all rights. It has been a love of country inspired by the free expression of these differences in thousands of forums and in hundreds of thousands of books from the distilled wisdom of which there has finally evolved this great economic and political system that stands as living testimony to the concept of freedom of thought and expression.

I cannot bring myself to believe . . . that now suddenly and overnight our children are in danger from the books they have been reading and the ideas they have been discussing. It is not the books they have been reading that disturbs me so much as the books they have not been reading. I hope that we have not come to the point where we equate all differences of opinions with subversion and let fear upset our capacity to make rational judgments.

. . . For what all of this represents is essentially a distrust of the intellectual and an attack on the processes of learning. You who ally yourselves with the world of books must know better than anybody else that in this age it is the educated man and woman who must see us through.

This is the last moment in our history when we should be fearful of what our bookshelves bear. Living as we do in a world which is so drastically on the move that our mental faculties are taxed to take note of the changes about us, much less to understand all of them, we only make more inadequate our capability to comprehend by limiting the area of legitimate inquiry. Our task is to challenge, to inspire, to motivate—and we cannot get this job done effectively if we spend our time and energy in picking our way through every book our students read to see if everyone agrees with every statement in it. What kind of soft-headed adolescents would our citizens be if they were spoon-fed every milk-toast bite that they ran through their intellectual craw? What we need in today's world is the tough-minded, intellectually disciplined individual who may not know all the answers but who does know the questions and who understands that neither is apt to be very simple—who is not afraid to explore new ground, knowing with Jefferson that no generation ever has a monopoly on truth.

What should concern us is not that our boys and girls may at some point be exposed to controversy but that they not recognize that which may legitimately be argued about. According to the limits that some would impose upon us, the subjects of some of the great debates of history would be eliminated from discussion. In any event the obvious effect of such a policy is to limit the pursuit of knowledge—in short to discourage the fullest quest for learning as represented by the classrooms of our schools. When we do this, we do not need to throw out our books—we just let them stay closed.

. . . Let me urge you . . . to retain our schools and libraries as the citadels of freedom and the defenders of the best of our heritage. Our teachers cannot teach and our children cannot learn in an atmosphere of suspicion and distrust. . . . We have, as we have always had, what I like to feel is a citizenry solidly loyal to this great country of ours and to its institutions. This is what our system of public education has produced without book censoring, without the intimidation of teachers, without dark hints of subversion.

. . . We must understand that this is an age for the development of ideas. This involves a process that we have tried to guard from the days of the great civilization that was ancient Greece—a process that insists on an exploration of the unknown, the untried, the difficult, the dangerous. This has been a technique that has invited dissent and disagreement.

. . . Ideas come from individuals and regardless of how large our system of education becomes or how massive the structure of our society, the development of the mind remains a private affair.

. . . In an age when it is increasingly difficult for a man to be himself, to hold to his own ideas, to live his own life, let us make of our great free system of education a more effective means than it ever has been before of bringing to our young men and young women a sense of individual worth and dignity and capacity. At a time when the concept of the "organization man" often seems to make a mockery of the words of Thomas Jefferson, may we remember that the "pursuit of happiness" is always an individual and frequently a lonely journey. But it is a journey which we must encourage more to make if they shall ever, in God's good time, find the way, the truth, and the life.

—"A Time for Thinking," speech, Phi Delta Kappa Education Fraternity, Jackson, Mississippi, March 19, 1964.

ON TECHNOLOGY AND GREAT BOOKS

As we look at a new generation far removed from the scenes of squalor and deprivation that I remember from my boyhood, where few had real access to formal education, we are facing another problem . . . the emergence of a technological society based on incredible advances in science and mathematics capable of creating machines that outperform the human mind. But in this process are we in danger of losing our souls?

. . . No one questions the amazing utility of these developments, as they make many of the daily tasks of living infinitely better. Through these miracles there now is available on our computer screens an array of information the like of which we have never known before. Much of the world's great literature can be called up with the flick of a button. But access and understanding are two different things. Just as television has been a much misused medium of information, we are in danger of letting computers become mere mechanical gadgets that divert us from the opportunity to enhance our humanity. . . . How do we preserve our essential humanity in the face of our increasing reliance on technology?

. . . Now we are called on to create out of this new information age . . . a cultural imperative that will preserve our common humanity. We can either let all this technology destroy our human-ness or we can employ it to enhance our ability to lead more fulfilling lives. But it can never take the place of reading.

There is no software package that I am aware of that automatically affirms the strength and resilience of the human spirit—only great literature can do that. That presses into our consciousness the values of fairness and decency and honor that we must live by—only great literature can do that. That delineates what is permanent and worth saving from that which is cheap and superficial—only great literature can do that. That causes us to contemplate the purpose of our living and the meaning of our existence—only great literature can do that. For these are truths that can be found only in the assimilated thinking and writing of those whose insights and experiences span every era of human history.

. . . Now we have so many more people with unlimited access to information who have no clue as to how to sort out the intellectual riches which are at their disposal. But unless we learn how to apply this age-old wisdom to the problems that confront us, we shall live in a society that will be increasingly divided and dangerous.

For the irony is that even though we have put behind us so much of what terrified us in the struggle with Communism and have achieved this incredible level of material affluence and productivity that we once thought would automatically produce a good society, we are finding instead a disturbing lack of civil discourse, mindless acts of violence, and a growing skepticism about the future. And so in our frustration we quit talking rationally to each other and retreat into little enclaves living in fear of our neighbors and our neighbors living in ignorance of us.

This is where we must call into play the collected wisdom and inspiration of those who have shared and recorded so much of human experience and who, if we will only listen, will help us to avoid the nightmare . . . that once was too often our common fate.

These fountainheads of wisdom cannot be reserved just for the bastions of the intellectual. They must be made a part of the currency of the marketplace. Good reading must be as common in these parts as good writing. Why can't we let literature and culture and civility be what people first think about when they think about our state and region—not our historic propensity for defiance and confrontation?

At a time when meanness and greed and self-centeredness make life less pleasant and satisfying for so many, when a lack of concern for the feelings of others is manifest in so many ways and when an impersonal social order squeezes the joy out of much that we are involved in, why can't we rely on a renewed appreciation of reading to lift us to a higher level of satisfaction and fulfillment?

And what is wrong with letting writers like Eudora Welty help us reaffirm our values and our virtues? . . . Why can't we let Eudora Welty and Willie Morris and Barry Hannah and Richard Ford and the two Walkers, Alice and Margaret, and those other great Southern writers speak for us instead of those brutish voices that create hate and division and alienation?

. . . This must then be our continuing commitment—to see that in these more affluent times we not let our pursuit of the fast buck or the superficial gain obscure the longer-range goals that should guide our society. That will not be easy to do. It gets harder and harder to know where our duty lies—what the right priorities are. But the models are there, molded and shaped in the pages of a thousand great books. It is there that we find the vision and the strength to see us through life's complexities and ambiguities and tragedies. We must insist that more of our fellow citizens join us on this incredible journey. . . . We all need to listen to the poet's voice.

—"Literature and the People," speech, Conference for the Book, University of Mississippi, April 12, 1996.

ON LIBRARIES

For where else in this frighteningly confused time in which we live can we find the voices that speak to us to give direction and meaning and inspiration to our lives? How otherwise could we come to know the courage, the compassion, the common sense that have served other men in other times and which we so desperately need in ours?

It has been in the seeming obscurity of the libraries of our land that more often than not we have received the security that has helped to mark our way. There are many voices that have spoken to us—voices that spoke out of other troubled times—voices that were not always sure—voices that were not always right—voices that frequently made no pretense at authority—but voices that nevertheless for many of us have softened our hearts and made more understanding our minds as we, too, have come groping along through the mists of life. These are voices that may not have been heard but for the libraries which have guarded them and held them for us.

. . . This is a time when these voices . . . must be recalled by more of us if men not only in Mississippi but throughout the world will be able to understand themselves and each other. The geographical frontiers, of this planet at least, are gone. The only frontiers that are left are those of the mind and heart. Man has learned to live on the land, to overcome the physical problems of survival with nature, to gain dominion over the sea and the air, to climb the highest mountain, to sail under the polar ice cap, to approach the stars.

But our survival as human beings is threatened at this hour as never before for the simple reasons that man has not yet learned to live with himself. Because greed and lust and selfishness and ignorance have barred the way to this last frontier, we find ourselves and our institutions on the threshold of destruction.

. . . What, then, can we say to each other . . . that will make sense in a society beset with so many troubles? We can say, first of all, out of the understanding which you who associate

with books possess more than I, that this is no time for despair.
You, I hope, would be able to place in the proper perspective
of history these events of recent weeks and know that out of
similar trials of the past have emerged stronger, wiser men.
But it is not enough that we be merely hopeful. We must
know, too, that for each of us there comes a time when we
must give affirmative voice in support of that in which
we believe and for which we stand. In times like this the
moment of truth may come for some of us with stark and
shocking force, as it already has for some of our fellow
Mississippians and fellow Americans. We stand up in these
hours of crisis only as we have access to the spiritual and intellectual resources available to us in books. It is only here that
we have distilled for us the accumulated experience and wisdom of the ages, pointing for each of us the way. It is when
we deliberately ignore these guideposts that we invite our
destruction.

. . . Our responsibility . . . is the sober one of seeking to
avoid at this juncture in the history of mankind the unhappy
process of plunging our world, our nation, our state, once more
into darkness. This is a struggle that finds us fighting a battle
against tyranny abroad and against conformity at home. This is
a time when there is almost a fanatical insistence on the part
of some men in owning the minds and souls of other men. The
practitioners of this art are particularly adept at the technique
of converting the half truth into the big lie—of transforming a
man's fears and prejudices into the dogma of his faith—of confusing self-interest with wilful self-destruction. It would appear
that the task of some of us is to try to keep our attitudes and
those of our colleagues in the perspective of reality.

We must continue to understand, therefore, that there
are no short, simple, easy solutions to our dilemmas, and
those who hold out black and white answers to most of our
problems do so without any real conception of the complexity

of the problems. We must face up to the sobering realization that there may not be in our lifetime the final solution to many of the difficulties, foreign and domestic, that now rise to plague us, but that does not render any less certain the responsibility that descends to each one of us to defend the processes of learning whereby man can seek to understand himself. We must remember that in this century in which we are living man's capacity for destroying has kept pace with his capacity for learning, and that if we are effectively to guard against the elements of destruction, we must do so by protecting the facilities of learning.

—"A Time for Responsibility," speech, Mississippi Library Association, Greenville, Mississippi, October 27, 1962.

Let us let this library stand as a living testament to the role of ideas in the shaping of a good community. Let us not be intimidated by those who themselves are threatened by ideas. The great hope for our free society is that it be able to preserve the opportunity for the far-ranging mind to challenge the rest of us. We can do this only as we have access to books.

. . . The real significance lies in the fact that the people of this area understand the priority that we have to place on reading and learning if we are to live properly. In this world of the late twentieth century, it is the individual who can think who will get ahead, and it is the country that can produce the most real thinkers who will lead the world.

As life comes to be more than just making a living, more than just surviving for more people, and at the same time as more of us live closer and closer together on this planet, we are faced with the biggest frontier yet—that of learning to live together. This may well be the greatest role yet for the public library.

—Found on the back of an old envelope probably written in route to a library dedication. Located in the personal papers in the William F. Winter Archives and History Building.

ON READING

My parents were both avid readers. And our home, modest
by today's standards and lacking radio or electricity or indoor
plumbing, nevertheless had a bookcase filled with great
books. It was out of this early association with reading at
home plus the encouragement of inspired teachers in my
school years . . . that I came to regard writers with the same
affection that I lavished on my sports heroes like Dizzy Dean
and Schoolboy Rowe.

. . . But in the past and still today this inspiration from
books could come only for those capable of, or at least inclined,
to read them.

. . . What I did not fully understand then but that I have
since come to comprehend much more clearly is that for so
many people—black people and white people alike—living and
growing up in the rural South in generations gone by, there
were these walls imposed by poverty and ignorance and class
and race that left thousands of them marooned in permanent
intellectual isolation and deprivation. A few escaped but so
many did not.

It has been an appallingly slow and tortuous journey out
of that dark hole. . . . Even today you can walk down the roads
and streets of almost any of our small towns and rural communities, and at least one out of every five adults you meet will be
functionally illiterate.

. . . There is a strange and haunting paradox about all of
this. In a state and region that has for so long prided itself on
its commitment to taking care of its own, on sustaining strong
family values, on helping each other, we tended to neglect that
most essential of all our social responsibilities, and that was
the extension of adequate educational opportunity to all of our
people. And there is an even stranger and more intriguing paradox. In this state where for so long so many have lacked the

very basic learning skills, we have produced such a disproportionate number of celebrated writers.

—"Literature and the People," speech, Conference for the Book, University of Mississippi,
April 12, 1996.

ON RALPH WALDO EMERSON

It was almost by accident that I discovered Emerson. Miss
Turner [high school English teacher] was not happy with my
recitation one day. She thought that I had been reading too
many baseball stories. If I was to return to her good graces she
informed me, it would be only after I had read and reported on
"Self-Reliance." So on a lovely fall weekend more suited to
hunting squirrels in the nearby woods than plodding through
the dusty tomes of a long-deceased New England essayist,
I reluctantly found a new and challenging world.

In an era when young people growing up in Mississippi
were not encouraged to embrace different ideas, I found
Emerson encouraging me to be a nonconformist. At a time
when one dared challenge the old shibboleths at his peril, I was
reading that "nothing is at last sacred but the integrity of our
own mind." When the admonition of my elders and the pressure of my peers combined to dictate what was acceptable, I
was being told by this Yankee from Massachusetts that I must
trust only myself.

Nothing that I had read before had had such a profound
and direct effect on my thinking. It was the beginning of my
education. Emerson, in a simpler time, helped prepare me for
the infinitely more complex world in which I would spend my
life. His essays defined more clearly than anything else that
I had ever read the process of sorting out the ideas we live
by—of deciding what to keep and what to throw away—
of testing what is proven and what is false. It is through the

establishment of this value system that we really find out who we are, and it is also the means that decides our relationship with everybody else.

Emerson seemed to be writing particularly for my generation of young Southerners growing up in the middle of the Great Depression where hope and optimism, fired by Roosevelt's New Deal, were then beginning to replace the stolid conformity of the past. He asked the right questions. Why were we so timid and imitative and compliant? Why did we look backward so much to the so-called good old days? Why did we automatically fear and thus resist change? Why did we cling to a herd instinct that was based on nothing more noble than mere survival?

"Self-Reliance" was an affirmation of faith in America. It was an affirmation of a commitment to the here and now and to the opportunity that the future held. It was not, however, an advocacy of the selfish and superficial trends that tended to mark America's later society. Emerson was writing primarily for the young idealists of his day, but he was really writing for the young at heart of every generation.

He put in perspective the temptations for selfish gain in calling on his readers to eschew a vulgar, self-directed prosperity in raising to a national cause freedom of thought and action. His essay was almost like the quiet admonition of the commander before the charge on the battlefield. He stressed the difficulty of the task, but underlined it with the glory of the achievement. There would be weariness, insult, misunderstanding, and failure, but the reward would be the exhilaration of living in a truly satisfying way.

He wrote of the tenacity that is required in sticking to the accomplishment of a worthy purpose. Life was not a voyage for the short-winded or the faint-hearted, and there would be no easy victories or at least no meaningful easy victories. Even the ones we did win would ensure no permanent happiness. External achievement did not guarantee internal contentment.

. . . Emerson's insistence on aspiring to standards of performance, of morality and of taste above the commonplace has special meaning, particularly in light of today's emphasis on the commercially driven establishment of what is popular and acceptable. In this era of television commercials, which subtly and often not so subtly suggest what we should wear, eat, drink, put on our hair, and make us irresistible to the opposite sex, it is helpful to be reminded of Emerson's rejection of mediocrity and blind conformity.

He calls for an elevation of private responsibility. His highest aspiration for the nation was the development of a broad-based citizen leadership that would by its own high standards of performance and example create a national commitment to excellence.

. . . The essay on "Heroism" follows in the same vein. It is an appeal to a quality of living that is based on "an obedience to a secret impulse of an individual's character." Like "Self-Reliance," it cries out to the idealism of young people to forego the easy standards and conventions of society and look to a more exciting and challenging course.

. . . One of the most novel and yet valuable pieces of advice that this essay contains addresses the problem confronted by all of us at times as we weigh our choices. The most inhibiting aspect of many decisions revolves around the concern of how we shall be perceived if we fail. We guard jealously our dignity lest we appear foolish. "Nonsense," responds Emerson.

. . . Another example of the heroic figure which he cites is that of one who is not ostentatious in his heroism. He simply is oblivious to both the plaudits and the criticism of others. His motives provide their own reward.

Temperance is the mark of the hero. Although he does not come across as a fanatical and solemn reformer, Emerson commends the person who does not require the stimulus of tobacco, drugs, or strong drink.

. . . Emerson argued against the folly of attempting to impose our form of government on other nations. He warned against the cult of personality in the selection of political leaders. . . . He called for this country to set an example for the world by putting the advancement of learning and commerce ahead of arms and military force. A complete idealist, he suggested a totally revolutionary idea in a world that in the century that would follow would see the most savage and deadly wars in history. His proposal: "The power of love, as the basis of a State, has never been tried." But he also understood why it had not worked. "For according to the order of nature, which is quite superior to our will, it stands thus; there will always be a government of force where men are selfish."

. . . Emerson insisted that if his proposal of a political system based on love and brotherhood could work, it would be the basis of achieving our national destiny. . . . While distrustful of the political process and the politicians who pursued it, he recognized its noble and fundamental basis. "Governments have their origin," he wrote, "in the moral identity of men."

The genius of Emerson has been perpetuated in the thinking and writing of many others who have shared his thoughts and been inspired by his classic idealism. It is a distressing commentary on our own age that the forces that Emerson rallied against—the unthinking public judgments now made more pervasive by the indulgence of television—have rendered infinitely more difficult the maintenance of individually held values. Still he remains what he established himself to be in the mid-nineteenth century—a man of rare and profound understanding of the delicate and sensitive nature of the individual's relationship to himself as well as to all mankind. To read his works is to have a deeper knowledge of ourselves as we pursue our miraculous and mystifying journey.

—Speech, Hinds Community College, Raymond, Mississippi, on the occasion of a National Endowment for the Humanities–sponsored program, 1991.

ON LANGUAGE

One of the lessons that some of us who have been in politics
or have been lawyers or, maybe what is worse, have been
both, never seem to learn very well is to keep our language
simple. We have a fatal fascination with words—the more
and the bigger the better. The result is frequently a confusion
of meaning and a breakdown in communication. Maybe we
intend it to be that way. It has become almost an occupational
requirement in some high-placed government and military
circles. . . . I think it is increasingly incumbent upon us individually and collectively in the interest of preserving our
rightful heritage as literate citizens of this great democracy
that we unite together in a common bond of understanding
and declare in an unequivocal declaration our steadfast opposition to verbosity and obfuscation in every form and under all
circumstances.

—Television commentary, WJTV, Jackson, Mississippi, 1985.

ON HISTORY

We are all a part of a link in a continuing chain of people and
events that neither begins nor ends with us but that forms an
unbroken connection between all that has gone before and all
that will happen in the future. . . . Without that understanding
that only an appreciation of history can give us, we have a lot
of trouble picking our way through the uncertainties that these
changing times bring. That is why it is important that we come
together . . . to shore up and support the institutions that are
committed to sustaining and defining that history.

All of us in our respective states of Alabama and Mississippi
are fortunate in that we live in a region that has generally put
great stock in history. Sometimes in our nostalgic remembering

we have placed an unrealistic golden glow on our past, recalling in our imagination that which never was.

. . . This over romanticizing of our history is a pitfall which those who would be faithful to that history must help us avoid. We saw this tendency in the controversy over the Confederate flag in my state . . . where we almost fought another civil war over a symbol that meant different things to different people. Thus our state flag became a divisive emblem rather than a unifying one. It is one thing to be informed by history. It is another to be consumed by it.

This points up an important and legitimate role for latter day historians. We must be the guardians of the accuracy and integrity of the process by which we record and preserve the records of our past. We must never let the political intrigues and passions of the moment subvert that purpose. And we must never be afraid to protect the records of those events in our past of which we may not necessarily be proud. History must reflect our bad times as well as our good ones.

—Speech, Alabama Department of Archives and History, Montgomery, Alabama, March 14, 2002.

In a time when there is a tendency in some circles to revise our history to suit current trends, we must continue to be the guardians of the accuracy and integrity of the process by which we preserve the records of our past. We must never let the political intrigues and passions of the moment subvert that purpose. And we must never be afraid to protect the records of the events in our past which we might rather forget.

History must reflect our bad times as well as our good ones, our mistakes as well as our successes, our defeats as well as our victories. It is only through a clear and honest look at our past that we are able to find the basis now and in the future to make wise judgments that will keep us from repeating the mistakes of that past. We must in short learn to be instructed by history but not imprisoned by it.

... Only a citizenry which is properly informed by its history can avoid those blunders and excesses which make us less noble and less civil and less secure.

This is what must demand our best efforts—to call all of our people to an increased awareness of the duties of citizenship and to use our sense of history to build a fairer, a more just and a more stable society.

—Speech, dedication of the William F. Winter Archives and History Building, Jackson, Mississippi, November 7, 2003.

ON WORLD WAR II

Hundreds of thousands—literally millions—of farm workers left the farm for the first time, many of them to go into the military, to go all over the world, to live with people of various backgrounds, with entirely different customs from the segregated society of rural Mississippi. Many of them left to go into the defense plants, to make more money than they had ever dreamed of making hoeing cotton or picking cotton on the farms of Mississippi. It changed their whole perspective: their horizons were raised, and so they would never be the same, just as the state that they had left would never be the same.

The war brought into the state . . . numerous military installations, some very large military camps. Camp Shelby, with some 75 to 85,000 troops. Camp McCain, just south of Grenada, with approximately 30,000 troops, and Camp Van Dorn, down in the remote corner of southwest Mississippi, at Centerville, with about 30,000 troops.

It was a segregated army. The military units were not desegregated. There were white units and black units, but all on the same post, and they came from all over the country. They would get out of the post on weekends and go into the small towns. There were several serious confrontations involving black soldiers and white segregationist Mississippians. Duck Hill was the scene of a shootout on a summer weekend. In Centerville there were serious confrontations there between some of the black troops and some of the local citizens.

. . . Senator Bilbo, the militantly segregationist senator from Mississippi, said that "this just goes to show you that the mixing of Negroes and whites that has taken place as a result of the war is going to cause serious problems," and he predicted all sorts of dire results as a consequence of black soldiers going into the Army, seeing the rest of the world, and not being satisfied with the segregation that they would return to in Mississippi.

. . . I was in a training unit over in Alabama. I was a white officer in a black training regiment. All of the enlisted troops were black, from all over the country, and a new experiment was tried shortly after I reached that regiment in the fall of 1944. Black officers were integrated with white officers in this unit. It was the first time that had been done. Those of us who were white officers, who had grown up in a segregated society, were having the opportunity—and I considered it an opportunity—to get to know black people on a horizontal basis—on a basis of equality. We shared the same mess hall; we shared the same sleeping accommodations; we worked together, and we developed a new understanding.

—Lecture, Millsaps College, Jackson, Mississippi, February 1, 1989.

Now fifty years after the [attack on Pearl Harbor], . . . those of my generation remember with undiminished vividness the shock of that day. On that grim, gray afternoon none of us who listened by radio to the ominous news could comprehend the immensity of the effort that would follow, nor did we have an inkling of the changes that the world would undergo in the ensuing years. We did understand that our lives would never be the same.

The impact on almost every American was sharp and direct. For most of us who were at the right age it meant ultimate, if not immediate, military service. For a nation still recovering from the Great Depression it unloosed our previously underutilized productive resources in a way that literally put everybody to work.

. . . With victory finally assured after almost four years, it was the war's aftermath that wrought the greatest change. For us Mississippians who had never experienced life outside our largely provincial rearing, we learned of a larger and more complex world. That was particularly true for the thousands of black soldiers, sailors, and airmen who, even though serving in a largely segregated military, saw a less than segregated society for the first time. The GI Bill gave all of us access to an education that would have been beyond the financial ability of many of us to achieve.

More than anything else . . . we viewed our country in a new light. It was a heady time. Acknowledged as the leader of the free world, America seemed to have few limits. . . . There was a strong sense of wanting to use our new-found strength to create a better life than our forebears had known.

Now a half-century later many of us look back perhaps too nostalgically on what seemed then a time of great excitement and great adventure. We, however, must never forget the tragedy and heartache that the war brought to so many. We must also acknowledge the disappointments and unfulfilled dreams that we as a people have experienced in the intervening years. But through it all we must also understand that in spite of our many failings we are a freer and more just nation than we were a half-century ago. We must now somehow rekindle the spirit of unity and self-sacrifice that served us so magnificently then. Only that will sustain us through the eventful years that lie before us.

—"Reflections on Pearl Harbor," writings completed, 1991.

No one, of course, can ever be sure what ultimately would have happened if the [atomic] bomb had not been employed at that time. What is absolutely certain is that the two bombs that were dropped on Hiroshima and Nagasaki did with dramatic suddenness end the uncertainty about the Japanese surrender. What also appears certain is that by ending the war at that point, many additional lives on both sides were spared. If at this late date it is considered appropriate to second-guess Truman's decision to use the bomb, that second-guessing should be confined to the dropping of the second bomb. In retrospect, capitulation by the Japanese would probably have been accomplished by the Hiroshima bombing alone plus a threat to drop the second. But we must remember that those hectic days did not permit the luxury of purely dispassionate analysis. The powerful emotional forces that had sustained us in the desperate struggle for survival in the early years of a war that had begun by the surprise attack by Japan on Pearl Harbor could not be easily dismissed while Americans were still being killed in the continuing fighting.

. . . Without knowing then or even now what all of the facts were on which President Truman relied for his decision to use the bomb, I remain convinced that he made the right call at a time when none of us knew what the future portended. We can only hope that no future circumstance will cause us to have to make a similar choice.

—"A Veteran's View of the End of World War II," *Journal of Mississippi History*, 57.4 (Winter 1995), p. 312.

ON ABRAHAM LINCOLN

What do we owe Lincoln? He was neither for the North nor against the South; he was for the country as the last, best hope of earth. The illusion of individuality never trapped him. Justice for all with mercy for all—no man could be free otherwise.

Clearly, beautifully, he recognized the epic vision of
America. He was beyond Illinois. He was beyond Virginia.
With time, with patience, America would fulfill its mission;
no legal argument, no armies in the field must be stronger than
the decency of government and the dignity of man.

. . . What does Lincoln's life mean to us today? First of all
in spite of the most terrible abuse and criticism from those
who opposed him, he carried out duties with dignity and
humility—without bitterness, and he preserved this great
country of ours. This would be much less great a country
if it had been permanently divided. So we have the responsibility of helping keep this country together, too.

This involves most particularly our respect for the laws of
this country—we are Americans before we are anything else.
This means respect for and obedience to unpopular laws. This
means giving to every other person the same sort of respect that
we want to receive. This means making sure that we are helping
to solve our country's problems and not contributing to them.

We have a great country, and as Mississippians, you and I
must act as a part of it. We can contribute too much to America
to be isolated from it.

—Speech, delivered on Lincoln's birthday, early 1960s.

ON HUBERT HUMPHREY

In the spring of 1968 . . . a group . . . at the University of Mississippi had invited him to the campus to make a speech.

. . . For many of us in the South it was not a very happy
time as the old ghosts of the past continued to haunt and distort
our politics and our relationships. It seemed that the bugaboos
of race would forever divert us from the tasks of educating all
of our people and leveling the paths to economic opportunity
and creating strong communities where everyone could live

in harmony. Strange as it may sound now, those were not the highest priorities in my state at that time. Most politicians spoke more about what they were against than what they were for. And what and whom they thought they were against was personified for most of them by Hubert Humphrey.

But on this bright May morning this much maligned man . . . serving as Vice President brought a message that the people of my state had rarely heard. It was a message of faith in the basic good sense of the American people and of optimism about our future. We had heard for so long the divisive and false cries of the doomsayers who had convinced so many of my fellow Southerners that the sun would stop coming up in the morning if segregation of the races should end.

But here was this man from Minnesota telling us that everybody would be better off when those old barriers of race came down.

. . . I would say today on behalf of my fellow white Southerners about Hubert Humphrey's speech what I once told Myrlie Evers, the widow of the fallen martyr, Medgar Evers . . . that her husband had done as much to free us white folks as he had to free black folks. And while we did not recognize it at the time, we can now look back and see that Hubert Humphrey helped to free us, too—from our fears and prejudices and doubts—from our reluctance to embrace change—from our defense of the indefensible.

From the vantage point of fifty years of history I must tell you that in the context of the time in which it was made, that speech by Hubert Humphrey was one of the most remarkable of the age. He made it not only against the obvious protests of the white South but against the cautious advice of many of the party's national leaders. This was no time they said to risk losing the southern base. What too many of my southern friends did not understand was that we were the ones at risk.

But it was more than a political battle that we were losing. It was a moral and spiritual battle as well. And no white leader in America understood that any better than Hubert Humphrey.

But despite his idealistic fervor and his insistence on standing on the principles in which he believed, there was no meanness or bitterness in Hubert Humphrey. He was one of those rare human beings who was unable to bear a grudge even though he was obliged to endure moments of deep and painful disappointment in his quest for the presidency. He bore with magnanimity and wry humor the hostility and insults that were frequently directed his way. While taking his cause seriously, he never took himself too seriously. He was, indeed, the "Happy Warrior."

What is not understood by many is that while obviously Hubert Humphrey had a considerable ego, as what person in politics does not, he had the ability to suppress that ego for the attainment of worthy goals. There are many examples—from the Peace Corps to disarmament to the monumental Civil Rights Act of 1964—where, in the interest of getting the legislation passed, Humphrey saw to it that others received the principal credit for his original initiatives.

And so today I have traveled a thousand miles up the valley of the great river that ties our two states together to join you in remembering this great American patriot to whom we all owe so much. Just as this river continues its inexorable journey to the sea, the majestic message of Hubert Humphrey which challenged us in our youth continues to fire our conscience and to remind us of the unfinished business which is before us.

—"Remembering Hubert Humphrey," speech, St. Paul, Minnesota, June 24, 1998.

ON SENATOR JOHN STENNIS

The qualities that have set him apart throughout his remarkable career as a state legislator, district attorney, circuit judge,

and senator have been his unquestioned integrity, his superior intellect, his fantastic capacity for work, and his total
dedication to the public interest. His unshakable faith in this
country and its political system has remained incredibly free
of personal self-interest and cynicism. Even as he was bringing reason and conciliation and common sense to the solution
of many of our grave national problems, he never forgot his
responsibility to be the spokesman and indeed the servant of
that vast number of people who have no effective voice except
their solitary individual vote.

—Television commentary, WJTV, Jackson, Mississippi, 1985.

Some of them [judges] were truly notable and were destined
for roles of historic leadership in the future. I would include in
that number Judge John Stennis, who as a visiting judge from
another circuit made an indelible impression on me as he held
court in Grenada County. I was only a first-year law student
but I was so inspired by this little known judge from DeKalb
that over fifty years later I can still recall his charge to the
grand jury on that summer morning.

He painted for those jurors—most of them farmers and
small businessmen of modest means—a picture of the sanctity
of the law, the nature of our system of justice, and the vital role
which they had to play in maintaining the integrity of that system. I knew then that I was in the presence of greatness, and
years afterward when he had become a United States Senator
and was being favorably mentioned for appointment to the U.S.
Supreme Court, I remembered his performance in that Grenada
County courtroom. He would, indeed, have been a worthy
member of the nation's highest tribunal.

—"Honoring the Judges," The Judge William C. Keady Distinguished Lecture Series V, Hinds
County Bar Association Meeting, Jackson, Mississippi, May 4, 2000.

MISSISSIPPI AND THE SOUTH

Gubernatorial candidate Winter with Chastain Junior High students, Election Day, November 1979.

ON THE SOUTH AND SOUTHERNERS

Two Souths . . . One is represented by the popular image of the modern Sunbelt—a region of burgeoning cities, high-wage, high-tech industry and the good life. This South embodies the bright fulfillment of long-held hopes and dreams—of the final coming together of those elements of destiny that would make this America's promised land. In contrast there is another South—still largely rural, agrarian, undereducated, under-productive, and underemployed—where life remains for too many a continuing malaise of frustration and unfulfilled expec-tations. Unless we act with wisdom and dispatch, we shall condemn our region to a permanent pattern of unequal oppor-tunity, development and achievement.
—Television commentary, WJTV, Jackson, Mississippi, 1985.

A special hazard in the interpretation of Southern history is the separating of myths from realities. We Southerners have always been infatuated with myths. One of our most persistent myths has been that we could build a competitive economy on a foun-dation of low wages, minimum education, and racial discrimi-nation. And if we have played games with what never was, we have to an even greater extent tended to fantasize about what is to be.

Another myth, born in the halcyon days of the seventies, proclaimed that our time had finally come in the South—not just for some of us, but for all of us. And with virtually the same

assurance that we had waved the banner of "segregation forever" a generation earlier, we announced in the mid-seventies
the official opening of an era of unparalleled prosperity, one that
would embrace not only the Atlantas and Orlandos, but also all
the little towns and rural counties in between.

—"Shadowboxing," *Southern Magazine*, October 1986.

When the Commission on the Future of the South met in
Atlanta . . . we asked Governor Bill Clinton of Arkansas to
appraise where we were starting from. The governor gave us
our direction in a line that was to become the subject of our
report. He said, "We're halfway home and a long way to go."

. . . I ask . . . how do we get all the way home? And when
I ask that question, I do not ask it for some of us. I ask it for all
of us. This is the heart of the problem. Not enough of our fellow Southerners have been making the journey. Some have not
even been starting it.

As long as I can remember, going back to the days of the
great depression when I was growing up on a hill farm in
Grenada County, I have been appalled by the abuse of our
resources. I remember the eroded, gullied land that had once
been productive, the stripped and slashed forests of South
Mississippi, the clogged and polluted rivers that smelled of
chemicals and creosote. But what I particularly remember
are those blank and empty faces of a generation of young
Mississippians—black and white—whom I knew as a boy and
whose lives have been stunted and dwarfed because they did
not have access to a basic education.

. . . We are now only halfway home because we were unable
and in too many instances unwilling to make the investments
in human resource development—in human capital formation—
that would have made a difference.

—"Halfway Home—How Do We Get the Rest of the Way?" speech, Millsaps College, Jackson,
Mississippi, February 21, 1989.

We Southerners must resolve that the way to get all the way
home is by investing more of our resources in the interdepen-
dent lives of our fellow Southerners.

—Speech, Leadership Florida, Orlando, Florida, March 24, 1990.

We know the difficulty of defining a region that has produced
so many paradoxes. I would cite the case of one of my own
great-grandfathers, a Union Whig who vigorously opposed
secession. Sensing the tragedy that was to follow, he reluctantly took up the cause of the South after Fort Sumter, and at
the end of the war, his spirit crushed and his fortune wasted, he
slowly set about to put his world back together. On the other
hand, there was my fire-eating grandfather who, after his surrender at Gainesville, Alabama, came out of the war as defiant
and militant a secessionist as ever. In those chaotic days after
the surrender the family on both sides accepted his marriage
to my grandmother, the daughter of the Union Whig, with the
same equanimity that they had endured the four years of war.

I was in Chattanooga a year or so ago when my host told me
of a breakfast appointment that he had arranged for me with
the administrative assistant to the mayor. It turned out to be a
black man whom I had known years before in North Mississippi
where we had grown up on adjoining farms. That, of course, had
been in the days of segregation, but in that rural farming area
the fact that we couldn't go to school together did not keep us
from swimming together in the creeks and lakes or hunting rab-
bits together or playing endlessly together the boyhood games
that were a part of those tranquil days. Only as we grew older
did we have to part company—he and I to go separately to a segregated army in World War II to fight a common enemy.

And as we ate together there in Chattanooga's finest hotel
on a bright autumn morning, where twenty-five years before
we could not have sat together regardless of how close our
friendship had been, my black companion reminded me of

170

where we both had come from. His grandfather had been born a slave on my great-grandfather's place—on the farm of the Union Whig who had opposed secession. His grandfather, as a slave boy, had played in the fields with my grandfather, until my grandfather, the fire-eating Confederate, had ridden off as a sixteen-year-old to fight with Forrest in defense of slavery.

How then can we possibly define and describe this region of such incredible paradox? Even for those of us who have grown up in this enchanted yet tormented land, it defies our full understanding.

—"What South Are We Talking About?" speech, Samford University, April 27, 1992.

Intertwined in our genes and in our psyches are the accumulated experiences of a region that more than any other has known both grandeur and poverty, triumph and defeat, selflessness and brutish greed.

. . . The paradoxes still abound. The South is the place where the greatest pride is taken in family and personal relationships. Yet it is also the place where still live the greatest number of underdeveloped and dependent human beings in the nation. It is a region that combines an abundance of all of the basic natural resources . . . that should make it the country's richest area. The fact is that it is the poorest. It is the place that has produced some of the world's greatest writers and literary figures. Yet we have the greatest number of functionally illiterate adults. . . . The South is the section that has most fiercely resisted change. But it is also the region that in recent years has been most drastically affected by change.

. . . For it has in fact been a part of our experience that we have painted for ourselves the giddy vision of a region without limits, and then we have proceeded to impose our own limits. This is the cruelest paradox of all.

. . . The time has now come in this almost mystical region— so often misunderstood and maligned by those among us who do not understand the paradoxes of our past—to put aside those forces that have separated us from our destiny.

. . . As long as there are still so many poor children and ill-housed families and uncompleted educations and misguided and misplaced lives, the New South still will not have arrived. In spite of the mistakes and missed opportunities of the past, in spite of the abuse of our natural and human resources, in spite of all of the elements that have separated us from the rest of the world and from each other, the South remains a region of incredible vitality and strength.

—Speech, Southern Growth Policies Board, Atlanta, Georgia, December 10, 1992.

The South is the nation's most complex region whose past is frequently misunderstood not only by many outside the region but by many of us Southerners ourselves. We could go into almost any community in the South . . . and depending on whom we talked to, we would get vastly different—even opposite—portraits of the region. Some would speak wistfully of a South of romantic legend—of great plantation houses and magnolias in the soft moonlight. But there would be others just down the road a piece who would speak of a South of poverty and ignorance and deprivation—a South of harsh and haunting memory.

. . . Political democracy for the white man and racial discrimination for the black were products of the same dynamics. The rise of Jim Crow laws was in almost direct proportion to the surge of popular democracy among the whites. Equally as paradoxical was the contrast during this period between the quest for a strict legally controlled social structure and a continued propensity for violence. The Old South had obviously been a violent place. The New South was more bloody.

. . . Most Southerners—that is to say most white Southerners—were resistant to change and certainly to any change that threatened the racial status quo.

. . . We must now learn from our history and decide once and for all what we want this New South to be. This is not a task for the quick-fixers and short-winded. It is not a task for the turf-protectors and self-promoters. It is not a task for the cynical critic or the naive idealist.

What it will require is resourceful planning, unselfish dedication, and plain old hard work. It will require our best minds and our most farsighted vision. And what it will require most of all is our ability and commitment to work together to achieve the goals that are larger than ourselves. Then we can say with reassurance and satisfaction that the long-promised New South has finally arrived

—Speech, Montgomery, Alabama campus of Auburn University, October 30, 1993.

It has been this overzealous concern with the maintenance of an indefensible social and political system that has caused us the most grief. What we need now is an understanding of what it is that we must be intent on preserving—of what is valuable and irreplaceable and what sets us apart in the right kind of way.

This may be the greatest contribution the South will have made to our larger society. For at a time when meanness and greed and selfishness make life less gratifying and satisfying for so many in our nation, when a lack of concern for the feelings of others is manifest in so many ways, and when an increasingly technological society is squeezing the humanity out of much of what we are involved in, we Southerners can take renewed inspiration from our emphasis on civility and graciousness and common courtesy that . . . have been a distinguishing characteristic of our section of the country.

What is wrong with us Southerners keeping an appreciation for the times and places and people that have shaped our lives and given us our values and our virtues?

. . . Sensitivity to the needs and feelings of our friends and neighbors may not be unique to the South, but it is one of the region's most enduring qualities. It is a part of our heritage which must not be lost or diminished.

What is wrong with us in this region that has produced some of the world's greatest literature and music and art letting those contributions to society be the elements that people first think about when they think about the South—not our historic propensity for guns and violence?

Why can't we let Eudora Welty and Leontyne Price speak and sing for our region instead of those voices that create only division and misunderstanding?

Why can't we do what Flannery O'Connor only half jestingly suggested, and that is let culture be our money-crop?

. . . And what is wrong with the South now at long last taking advantage of its rich resources of human and physical capital to create a higher standard of living for more of its people and seeing to it that nobody gets left out?

. . . None of this means that the South need give up its distinctiveness. What it may mean on the contrary is that the South may finally be able to put behind it the elements that were its worst characteristics and now bring to the fore the qualities that have been its strengths. That would be a great advance not only for the South but for the nation.

. . . The South will continue to be the South only as we insist on preserving our sense of community, only as we not forget our history, only as we, in recognizing our increasing multicultural diversity, understand and celebrate our common humanity.

—"What Is Southern about a Southern View," speech, North Carolina Center for the Advancement of Teaching, January 14, 1995.

Southern politics . . . there was a Gothic quality to all of this, and many people regarded Southern politics as theater, as entertainment, at a time when in most rural communities opportunities for more conventional diversions were limited. In a region where the per capita income of the people was scarcely more than one-half the national average and when about the same percentage were functionally illiterate, it is no surprise that the politicians were able to play with great success on the frailties and foibles of the citizenry. Add to that the explosive factor of race, and the situation was fraught with the potential for all kinds of mischief.

. . . There are . . . two forces that continue to set the politics of the Deep South apart from the rest of the country despite all the changes that have taken place. One is the intense sensitivity of so many Southerners to the emotional social issues like abortion, gay rights, and school prayer. Those present-day issues are comparable to those heated controversies over prohibition and Sunday blue laws as political causes in the South in the last century.

The other factor is the one that has shadowed Southern politics since the first slave set foot in Virginia four centuries ago, and that of course is the politics of race. At a time when it was hoped that, after all that we have gone through, race would no longer matter politically, it unfortunately remains the issue around which we still seem to choose up political sides. Even though the rhetoric now is more civil and sedate, the racial fault line is still very much in evidence.

What we can say with assurance, though, and with understandable regional pride is that the South is a much more respected and influential force on the national political scene than it was. . . . The politics of the South seem to have matured. Maybe we have finally arrived.

—"The Evolution of Politics in the Deep South," speech, Natchez, Mississippi, February 25, 2004.

ON MISSISSIPPI

It is only through a process of self-evaluation and self-analysis that we make any real progress. . . . Our great potential . . . has

to do with a factor . . . which may well prove to be the most
difficult to do anything about. I refer to the matter of attitude—
to the building up among ourselves of a self-confidence based
on a realistic appraisal of the possibilities that exist for us.
We need to develop in this state a greater appreciation of the
promise that lies before us. I realize that we have come through
some rough years in this once exploited state. And out of the
experiences we have tended to express at times a rather militant inferiority complex that has manifested itself in ways that
have not always been helpful or becoming. We are no longer
a have-not state, though, and even if we have not achieved the
economic level that we aspire to, we are a long way down the
road from the tick-infested, boll-weevil-infested, sharecropper-
shackled state of a generation ago. Just because we have a lot
more to do doesn't mean that we can't appraise with a mature
and confident satisfaction what we have done. If there be those,
and I am convinced they are not as many as some would say,
who would criticize us, it does not necessarily have to mean
the refighting of the Civil War on our part. We are not com-
pelled to react with blazing indignation to every barb that may
be hurled our way. We must remove the defensive complex
that has made us too preoccupied with lashing back instead of
striking forward.

—"What's Wrong with Mississippi?" speech, Rotary Club, Jackson, Mississippi, August 22, 1960.

Mississippi has now reached the point in her history where
we must face the plain and sober fact that if we are to have
a proper share in the great adventures and opportunities of
today's world, we are going to have to junk some of the old
slogans and shibboleths that we have used for so long and substitute in their place a determination that nothing will be permitted to hold us back.

    . . . What do we find these days in so many of our fellow
Mississippians who ought to know better? Instead of a proud

and confident assurance that the best years in our state's history lie just ahead, they present an air of pessimism and foreboding and a wistful desire to go back to the good old days that, to tell the truth, weren't nearly as good as our nostalgic memories now make them out.

For my part, I want no more of those years of undereducated, underfed, and overworked people that still haunt my recollections. . . . And to those who would have us go back to the old have-not ways of inadequate schools, of poor roads, of gullied farms, I would remind them that we owe our children more than the second-rate lives that so many of other generations have been obliged to lead.

. . . The progress that is harder to measure but that is more important involves the state of mind of the people themselves. We cannot move as fast as we should until more citizens of our state have the vision of what our future can be like. Every man has a more or less vague aspiration for a better life for himself and his children, but too few are willing to lay aside old ways and outmoded concepts in order to share in the increased opportunities of tomorrow.

The task that we have then is to help lead more of our people to an understanding that the world is not coming to an end just because many changes are taking place with great rapidity about us. And instead of exhausting all of our energy in an effort at defending everything we have done for the last hundred years without regard to whether it needs defending or can be defended, let us spend our time more profitably by planning a program of accomplishment for the next hundred, or more realistically the next ten.

. . . Our state will move only under the impact of an educated citizenry—trained not only to hold a job but to live a life—trained not only to do but to think. The undeniable fact is that Mississippi can never move forward as far or as fast as it should as long as we still have many of our people who do not have an education adequate to match their needs as workers and as citizens. Even with a comparatively good education, it is all most of us can do to keep up with the pace of life as it is lived today. It is next to impossible for those without the floor of at least a high school education to compete on anything like satisfactory terms. . . . Let us make sure that we educate for more than the reading of a gauge or the turning of a switch. We also need men and women who understand the significance of their relationship to their communities, their state and their nation and their loyalties to all.

. . . The passions and prejudices of people must not be played upon, as if they were some musical instrument, for the cynical amusement or subtle purpose of anyone, and this most certainly includes political purposes. All of our citizenry capable of understanding must be given to know that our state will be, regardless of provocation or excuse, a place where the laws will be upheld and order maintained. This is not only right morally: it is essential economically. We can realize our full economic potential and find our place in the industrial sun only as we insist on the avoidance of internal strife. This, too, is a matter of leadership and attitude.

—Speech, Jaycees DSA Banquet, Vicksburg, Mississippi, January 18, 1965.

We now are beginning to have in Mississippi the opportunity to make up for some of the years that the locusts have eaten, when we did not have the capacity to develop our state fully even if we had had the inclination. Now that we have the capacity, we must make certain that more of our people have the determination. Our primary task then is to make certain that this pattern of growth and development proceeds apace, unimpeded and undeterred by either a fear for the future or a pining for the past. Here again it will be on the basis of performance that we will be judged. Let us then, each one of us, resolve that our energies will continue to be directed to a serious search for solutions to problems and not to their perpetuation; that our days will be spent in a girding for great achievement rather than in a brooding over lost causes; and that we reflect in our attitudes regardless of how trying the circumstances or how difficult the problems an unquench-able faith in the basic civility and ultimate decency of the vast majority of our fellow men.

—Speech, Annual Meeting of Mississippi Federated Cooperatives, August 5, 1965.

But there have been so many years that the locusts have eaten, when we still pitted ourselves against each other, white against black, rich against poor, businessman against farmer, the Delta against the Hills, South Mississippian against North Mississippian. We saw our beautiful soil stripped by erosion, our forests laid waste, our rivers run red, our great natural bounty wasted before our very eyes, and we wondered why we did not prosper.

We have wasted too much time. We have wasted too much of our substance. We have spent too many of our years, too much of our energy being against things we did not understand, being afraid of change, being suspicious of the intellectual, and being oblivious to our image and our reputation.

Now the time has come to get on with the job—long overdue—of building this state into the land of prosperity that it truly can be. . . . I believe with all of the fiber of my being that the remaining twenty years of this century belong to this area of America—to this great heartland of the Deep South—to this state beautifully and picturesquely named "Mississippi." Let those syllables roll off your tongue, with the assurance that this is where the action is going to be. . . . These will not be the years that the locusts have eaten. These will be the years of fulfillment and satisfaction and pride and accomplishment.

. . . We say to our sister states, "We have here what the rest of the nation is looking for—people who are willing to work—who don't want a free ride—who will settle for nothing less than a well-done job. We have here the resources essential to the building of a self-sufficient nation. Resources of energy— resources of food—resources of fiber—resources of shelter—all that in a benign climate, where the living is good, and more important than anything else, a good spirit in our people, where bitterness has been put aside, where people do not ask, "Where did he come from?" or "What club does he belong to?" or "What color is his skin?" The question they ask is "What can he do?"

. . . We cannot enjoy the luxury of letting up in Mississippi. We still have too much catching up to do. We have to run faster and get up earlier and stay up later to get to where we want to be. This will not happen because we want it to happen. . . . It will occur only as enough of us are willing to struggle to make it happen. I want us to stop selling ourselves short by not fully utilizing all of our people—our talented people—our creative and imaginative people. The old solutions will not do. Let us not be afraid to launch out into new areas. Let us not feel threatened by new ways of doing things.

—Inaugural Address, Joint Session of the Mississippi Legislature in the House of Representatives, Old Capitol, Jackson, Mississippi, January 22, 1980.

As I travel around this country, I find so many people viewing Mississippi now through different eyes. There has begun to develop something of a mystique about the state, as we have shed the old image of a people still living in the past. This new mystique is based on a perception of a state with a great history. . . . But it is also based on an understanding that this is a place that has not been cluttered up and spoiled by too much fast and uncontrolled growth and too much urban sprawl.

The result is the strange and appealing mystique that has this unique mix of the old and the new. It is the romance of Mississippi River steamboats, cast now as the nation's largest inland barge fleet. . . . It is the blending of a one-crop agricultural base into a mix so varied as to defy detailing—from cotton to soybeans to rice and wheat—from cows to chickens to catfish. It is a natural resource treasure trove of good earth and clean water—of all the basic energy sources—of the fastest-growing trees in the country.

. . . But this is still not what makes the mystique. These features only create the physical setting for the mystique. The mystique lies in those fantastic features of the people themselves. . . . At the risk of sounding chauvinistic, I am convinced that there is a unique quality to this fascinating mix of human beings that claim to be Mississippians. It is a quality that lay unrecognized for so many years under the inhibitions of a social system that generated for itself too many fears. Now with those fears dissipated and laid to rest, we can truly be ourselves and enjoy what so many other people in this country may have forgotten how to enjoy, and that is our common humanity.

—Speech, rededication of the Mississippi Capitol, Jackson, Mississippi, June 3, 1983.

Death came quietly in Hattiesburg this week to a distinguished native son. On tomorrow afternoon, former Governor Paul B. Johnson, Jr., will be taken to his final resting place beneath the longleaf pines of his beloved Forrest County. . . . The placid setting where he will be buried is in sharp contrast to the stormy and often violent times in which he lived. It was due in no small measure to his resolute and responsible leadership as governor that the tensions that marked the early 1960s were put behind us and that since those often grim days, Mississippi has been able to devote its energy to the economic and educational progress of its people. I had not voted for him in the primaries when he was nominated for governor. I was known as a Coleman man. But I had the personal good fortune to be a part of the Paul Johnson administration. My office as state treasurer was in the capitol building, only a few steps from the governor's office. I had applauded his eloquent inaugural address and his plea for racial harmony and understanding. In that four years, I saw how his quiet, low key approach to explosive situations was disarming our critics and winning friends for our state. No governor ever fought harder for Mississippi or tried to serve it more effectively, than this tall, almost shy, but always eloquent spokesman from the piney woods. No political leader ever had a more devoted or loyal following. Inheritor of a respected name from his own distinguished father, Paul B. Johnson, Jr., passes on to his family and fellow citizens, a legacy of accomplishment and service that will be remembered as long as the yellow pines stand tall in the South Mississippi sunshine, as long as there is a state called Mississippi.

—Television commentary, WJTV, Jackson, Mississippi, 1985.

The unhappy fact is that regardless of whether we deserve it, we have an image problem to overcome. We are called on now to recognize that the diminishing of that problem must be a priority for all of us. All of us must be involved in this process—not in a shallow chauvinistic way but in an effective showcasing of the positive change that has taken place throughout the state.

This really is how we shall get all the way home in Mississippi. We must turn away once and for all from that attitude that Hartley Peavy, the internationally successful Meridian industrialist, calls the "caboose mentality." By that he means that self-defeating, defensive, pessimistic appraisal of ourselves which in the past has so often been reflected in a kind of defiant inferiority complex. We no longer have to be haunted by a sense that we have been made the victims of a gigantic conspiracy that would relegate us forever to a place at the back of the bus.

But if we are going to drive the bus or at least occupy a seat reasonably close to the front, we are going to have to move toward the front together. That can't be done if the unseen

hand of Jim Crow still inhibits us. There are still too many disturbing instances of insensitivity to and even conscious disregard of the feelings and needs of many black people in our state.

All of the advances in education, employment, public
accommodations, and politics cannot obscure the less obvious
but nonetheless meaningful situations where additional progress needs to be made. There are, for example, very few blacks
to be found in any of the established luncheon clubs where
much public opinion is shaped and business relationships
are enhanced. While most white Mississippians are involved
increasingly in business transactions with their black counterparts, those relationships usually cease at the end of the working day. It is unlikely that many blacks have been entertained
or invited to dinner in white homes. There has been too much
white flight from the public schools. Even our churches have
been slow to extend more than a formal or perfunctory welcome to black visitors or communicants.

. . . We have always been a generous people, sharing sometimes what we did not have. Now that we have so much, let
us for goodness sake not fall into the trap of ignoring our own.
These are not obligations that we can casually pass on to others.
Let us increase our investment in education at all levels. Let
us dramatically reduce the rate of adult illiteracy and infant
mortality and juvenile delinquency and teenage pregnancy not
just by pious preachments but by recognizing that more than a
vague public responsibility is involved—that in our society that
obligation is also a personal one. I would urge us all to examine
what each one of us can do to change our state for the better.

—"Halfway Home—How Do We Get the Rest of the Way?" speech, Millsaps College, Jackson,
Mississippi, February 21, 1989.

Of all of the changes that have taken place in this state during
my lifetime one of the two most significant ones has been the
increased recognition of the importance of education in our

lives. The other has been the elimination of Jim Crow. These changes are now at the heart of our state's present economic progress. They are the forces that are moving us out of the backwaters of the past.

This would not have been possible if the people of our state had not accepted the reality that we could never prosper with a second-rate system of education and a policy of racial segregation. Looking back on the confrontational events of the fifties and sixties, I find it hard to believe now that we did not understand those facts then. But regardless of how it came about, the elimination of Jim Crow and increased support for education have been the most meaningful developments in the South in this century and have made it possible for this region to emerge now as a center of national political leadership and economic ascendancy.

—"Millennium Reflections," writings completed June 15, 1999.

ON THE STATE FLAG

As the grandson of a former Confederate soldier who once held me on his knee and told me of his experiences in the Civil War, I have a special appreciation of the history behind our old flag. I do not want to see that flag denigrated or maligned. Rather, I want to ensure that it is preserved and respected.

At the same time, I am convinced . . . that the old flag is a center of contention and controversy. I have always thought that a flag ought to symbolize unity and that everybody should be able to look at it and say with one voice, "That is my flag." Unfortunately, that is not the case with Mississippi's old flag, and it is creating tensions that will ultimately cost our state dearly in many ways.

So, in order to solve a problem that is not going to go away, I would propose that we do what people of common sense and good will usually do. I would suggest that we come together around some reasonable middle ground.

. . . I believe that we Mississippians are in a unique position to provide national leadership by using this situation with our flag to help bridge some of the gaps, largely along the lines of race, that continue to divide us not only in Mississippi, but in the country as a whole.

I would like to think that we have a special insight into how this can be accomplished. Having been the state whose history has been most shaped by the factors of race over three centuries, we may be best equipped to apply the hard-earned lessons of the past to resolving the problems of today. Not one of us, black or white, who has lived in the South in the last half-century is untouched by the memories if not by the actual experiences arising out of the trauma of racial segregation and the struggles that its demise precipitated. Let us hope that we are now through exhausting our energy on those old battles. Being instructed by history is one thing. Being consumed by it is another.

. . . What we need now is an understanding of what it is that we must be intent on preserving—of what is valuable and irre-placeable and what sets us apart in the right kind of way. There is nothing wrong with us Mississippians keeping an apprecia-tion for the times and places and people that have shaped our lives and given us our values and our virtues. It is only through what Eudora Welty has called a "sense of place" that we are able to establish our identity as to who we are and what we stand for.

. . . None of this means that we need give up our heritage. What it may mean on the contrary is that we may finally be able to put behind us the elements that were our worst char-acteristics and now bring to the fore the qualities that have been our strengths. That would be a great advance not only for Mississippi but for the nation.

—Speech, The Stennis Institute, Jackson, Mississippi, November 20, 2000.

ON MANNERS AND CIVILITY

Of all the qualities that we have prided ourselves on in Mississippi and the Deep South, none has been more heralded, and for good reason, than our civility, our courtesy, and our hospitality. These attributes have been for most of us a deeply ingrained part of our daily living, and in years gone by we came to regard an absence of those qualities in others as prima facie evidence of "bad manners" and, more than that, as certain proof of a foreign, or perhaps what was worse, a Yankee background.

The point is that as we lose our provincialism as a result of the greatly expanded relationships with other areas of the nation and the world, we owe ourselves and our descendants the obligation of trying to keep our civility. It is not necessary that we shed our manners at the same time that we reduce our prejudices. It is both desirable and possible that we adopt increasingly open and more tolerant attitudes toward new people and new ideas without succumbing to the vulgarity and offensiveness of much of the so-called pop culture and new morality.

—"The Ultimate Legacy," chapter in *Mississippi 1990*, published by University Press of Mississippi, 1979.

ON JEWS IN MISSISSIPPI

In retrospect I can find in my hometown of Grenada in the thirties and forties and fifties a microcosm of Jewish entrepreneurship and community leadership. All were highly regarded citizens, and if there was ever reflected toward them any anti-Semitic bias, I was never aware of it, although I can imagine that among some of the racist rabble, there may have been, especially in the sixties when some of the Klan type organizations began to emerge.

As I went off to Ole Miss I found there a group of Jewish students, many of whom became my closest friends. For the most part they came from the Delta towns like Clarksdale, Greenville, Vicksburg, and all of the other little places in between—places with colorful names like Rolling Fork and Anguilla and Tunica and Indianola. Their parents were almost always retail merchants. Their Ole Miss offspring were among the best and brightest on the campus.

. . . In the first fifty years of this century the places in the South for the best opportunity to develop small businesses with modest capital were in the little agricultural communities of the Delta and in the railroad towns like Meridian and Corinth and later Laurel and Hattiesburg. Now the little farm towns are struggling, and the sons and daughters of those wonderful old Jewish families have now gone like so many others to the metropolitan areas.

This is why it is so important for us . . . to reflect on the contributions to our culture that these great men and women have made. They were a special and hardy breed who knew the meaning of hard work, devotion to family, and commitment to their faith. Their heritage is sacred to us all.

—Speech, Museum of the Southern Jewish Experience, Utica, Mississippi, January 17, 1999.

ON THE BLACK MARKET TAX

The imposing metal warehouse was located a hundred feet off the gravel road. A closed panel truck and a trailer were parked by the side of the building. A dust-covered mail box indicated that the address was Casey's Lane, but the numbers had been either deliberately erased or worn away by years of exposure to the sun and rain. The building displayed no sign to indicate the nature of the activity that was being conducted there. Situated in the Pearl River flats several miles east of Jackson, this was an unlikely site for any sort of thriving commercial activity. Yet from the numerous tire tracks in the unpaved parking lot it was evident that there was considerable coming and going at this rural outpost.

"They unload the trailers in the back," my deputy, Clyde Pace, explained. He was introducing me to the never never land of the Mississippi liquor business. He thought I should meet the state's largest bootlegger, who was also the largest black market taxpayer. From his warehouse on Casey's Lane in Rankin County he was the principal supplier of the Capital City's lucrative clientele. He paid about twelve thousand dollars a month in taxes usually in crisp one thousand dollar bills. He did not want to be confronted later with a cancelled check bearing his signature.

I had never seen a warehouse stocked with a hundred thousand dollars worth of wine and whiskey before. The cases towered ten feet above my head as Clyde and I walked through the warehouse doors. The proprietor was a polite but reserved man who seemed pleased that I would pay him an official call.

By the mid-1950s Mississippi was one of only two states which still held to a policy of statewide prohibition despite numerous efforts at repeal. . . . It was obvious that a lot of whiskey drinking was going on despite a law that made it a criminal offense even to possess much less sell the minutest quantity of liquor. Only beer was legal, and that was on a local option basis. In most of the state's eighty-two counties public sentiment supported prohibition, although in some of those the local law enforcement officials were less than diligent in their enforcement of the law. Some sheriffs achieved a remarkable affluence that was hardly justified by their authorized salary.

In a few areas, notably on the free-wheeling Gulf Coast and in the old plantation counties along the Mississippi River, there was little effort to suppress the liquor sales. An over-whelming majority of the local populace supported this policy. A sheriff in these counties risked political retribution if he insisted on enforcing the prohibition law.

. . . In some counties there was less consistency. That called for ingenuity on the part of the bootleggers. In Greenville, where the city authorities were more diligent than the county sheriff in enforcing the law, one operator just outside the city had to keep moving his place of business as the city bound-ary lines were successively extended. After several frustrat-ing moves he finally jacked up his store and put it on wheels. His place became known around the community as the "The Rolling Store."

Another bootlegger had an establishment on the bound-ary between two counties. The county line ran smack down the middle of the store. The enterprising owner was thus able to keep his illicit stock on whichever side of the place was currently in favor with the sheriffs of the respective counties. The result of all this was a longstanding system of de facto local option that permitted vast quantities of liquor to be sold tax-free and without official regulation. The U.S. Treasury Department issued these unsanctioned sellers federal liquor licenses. In the year in which I became state tax collector there were 33 holders of federal wholesale permits and 914 holders of retail permits in the officially dry state of Mississippi.

Some members of the 1944 legislature including my father had thought that the state ought to do something about what was obviously a hypocritical situation. With a war on, black markets had sprung up involving the sale of consumer items that were in short supply—things like tires, cigarettes, and gas-oline. Accordingly a bill passed to discourage such unpatriotic practices by levying a tax on "the sale of any tangible personal property the sale of which is prohibited by law."

The word "liquor" was never mentioned, but it was discreetly understood that the law's main application would be directed at that product. It did not remove the criminal penalties for the sale of liquor. In fact, it provided that receipts for payment of the tax could be used as prima facie evidence of the breach of the prohibition law.

The principal source of supply for the Mississippi liquor trade was Louisiana. Large wholesale houses had sprung up in New Orleans and in the little river towns across the bridges from Natchez and Vicksburg. What was of special importance to us was the generous tax discount which the state of Louisiana granted on liquor purchases by federally licensed Mississippi dealers. Detailed records of such purchases were filed with the Louisiana Department of Revenue. Included in these records was such revealing information as the name and address of the Mississippi purchaser, the location of the place of business, and the route that the purchaser took in returning to Mississippi. In a remarkably cooperative effort with Louisiana, our office subsidized the salaries of two of their employees who provided us on a daily basis with copies of these detailed reports. Our state law required that the reports be made available to any law enforcement officer on request. We received few such requests.

One of the problems with which we were confronted was that while most of the purchases of the tax-discounted Louisiana liquor paid the black market tax conscientiously, a few were evading it. This not only meant lost revenue to the state, and incidentally to the collector, but it was a morale problem for the people who were trying to obey the law, or at least one of the laws. I determined to try to correct this inequity. I called a meeting in my office of the entire membership of the taxpaying bootlegging fraternity in Mississippi. It was a scene straight out of *Guys and Dolls*. They appeared for the most part to be typical hard-working businessmen such as would gather for a committee meeting at the chamber of commerce. As a matter of fact, some of them were active in their local chambers, civic clubs, and churches. They were eager to cooperate. The remedy for our common problem was obvious. I would request Louisiana to refuse to sell tax-discounted liquor to any Mississippi liquor dealer whom I did not certify as being in good standing. Louisiana was totally supportive, and our list of delinquencies was reduced to virtually zero. I had in effect become the licensing agent for the illegal liquor business in Mississippi. Tax collections increased perceptibly. Morale among the taxpayers was also up.

I felt that I should learn as much about the taxpayers as I could. That was when Clyde Pace and I decided to visit the warehouse on Casey's Lane. The proprietor was well known in the Jackson area. As the city's largest supplier of alcoholic beverages, he had a distinguished clientele. He provided special services for his better customers. This included home delivery if the order was as much as a case. As in any business there were occasional glitches. Once in a mix-up of addresses a large consignment of whiskey was left on the steps of one of the city's most zealous anti-liquor preachers.

Another of the problems unique to the business was the intermittent interdiction by the state highway patrol of trucks returning from Louisiana. Such an unhappy occurrence had recently befallen the proprietor at Casey's Lane. An entire load of liquor had been confiscated. The driver of the truck had been required to pay a fine. The proprietor requested that he be given a credit on his taxes for the state-imposed loss of his property. I was sympathetic but I had to turn him down.

"That is just one of the hazards of the occupation you are in," I told him. He seemed to understand.

Now as I stood in his place of business amid the stacks of his liquid inventory I recognized more fully how resourceful one in his vocation had to be. Without the protection of the law he was at the mercy of everyone from the governor to the local sheriff to the militant prohibitionists. I had heard that one such threatening problem emanated from the congregation of a newly constructed church a couple of hundred yards down the road and within sight of the warehouse where we stood. I inquired of the proprietor if this were a source of concern.

"It was at first," he conceded. "But I know the chairman of the building committee at the church. I told him I wanted to be a good neighbor, and I noticed the church needed some pews. I contributed the pews," he said. There had been no further trouble.

There were several wholesale dealers in Vicksburg, directly across the river from Tallulah, Louisiana, where major sources of supply were located. All of the Vicksburg stores seemed amply provided for. One of them was located directly in the middle of an area where a devastating tornado had swept through a short time before. I commented to the owner about how miraculous it was that his establishment had not been damaged when every building around him had been flattened by the storm. He assured me that, indeed, not one bottle of liquor had been broken. "How do you account for that?" I asked him. "I guess the Lord was just with me," he guilelessly replied.

Natchez was another center of activity. In the Delta, wholesale warehouses operated in Cleveland, Ruleville, Indianola, and Greenwood. In addition to the local needs, they supplied the considerable markets in the less visibly open counties of North Mississippi. The Coast, of course, was a huge market, and several wholesalers operated in Harrison and Hancock counties.

The hypocrisy of the situation distressed me. I had voted for statutory local option as a legislator. I was even more convinced now that the law ought to be changed. It was corrupting

a number of sheriffs and making it impossible for the law
to be enforced with uniformity or consistency. I also disap-
proved of the tax collector's office and said so at the time I was
appointed. I recommended abolishing it and turning over the
duties to the state tax commission, but the chairman of the tax
commission was opposed. He did not want to be involved with
the black market tax.

—Unpublished personal memoirs.

THE MEASURE
OF OUR DAYS

Winter with kindergarten students in Tupelo, Mississippi, September 1986. "The only real measure of the worth of our accomplishments lies in the extent to which our efforts make a difference for the better in the lives of our fellow human beings."

ON LIVING AND DYING

What enables us to cope more adequately with the death of friends and loved ones it seems to me lies in large measure in how well we have lived with them. It is in our living that we establish the measure of our dying. For most of us—maybe for all of us—the death of a friend or loved one is softened and made immeasurably more bearable by the recognition that our relationship has been free of the petty little envies and jealousies that in too many instances mar our lives and make more painful our dying.

And I am talking about not just the broken or strained personal relationships but the indifference and disregard for the needs of others at times when we could have served those needs but did not.

That is what marks the true pain of death. A few years ago I attended the funeral of a man with whom I had started to school in a little rural one-room schoolhouse a long time ago. He was a bright and attractive lad—one of my regular playmates. But his parents were poor sharecroppers. Uneducated themselves, they saw no need for their son to go to school, and so he dropped out in the fourth grade. In the intervening years he and I kept in touch, and when I ran for office he would always help me. But his life was one long battle for survival, and when we buried him in the little country cemetery, I felt a nagging pain that was not related to my friend's death but to his life. I grieved not that he had died but that he never had a chance to live.

A year or so later after that I attended another funeral . . . down the road from where I had grown up. It was the death of another friend—an African American a little older than myself. The family asked me to say a few words. I spoke of the qualities of character that enabled this man to rear ten fine self-respecting, successful children and to do it with the most meager resources that one could imagine. This wonderful black man, who lived most of his life in a rigidly segregated society and who was over forty years old before he was permitted to vote nevertheless retained somehow his sense of dignity and self-worth and instilled those qualities in his children.

At his funeral I felt again that nagging pain that came from the realization that this good man and so many like him had had to live so much of their lives weighed down by the artificial barriers that a harsh and insensitive segregated society had imposed on them. But there was also a joy in that little church that day that a life like his had been shared with so many of us who were there to pay our last respects.

And so this is the real measure of our approach to death. That we recognize that its pain will be enhanced or diminished by our own sense of how we have lived our lives in relation to others. This assessment cannot properly be limited to our individual relationships. We must grieve as a society over the broken and unfulfilled lives of so many of our fellow human beings, the tragedy and failure of which, in too many instances, all of us surely must bear some responsibility. Only in our true concern for the living can we soften our anguish in their dying. For we must remember that as the funeral bell tolls for our fallen comrades, it also tolls for each of us.

—"Reflections on Death and Dying," speech, Renaissance Meeting, Hilton Head Island, South Carolina, 1994.

The measure of the worth of the efforts of any of us is illusory at best. It cannot be accurately gauged by the amount of money we are paid or accumulate. It cannot be reflected in official positions held. It cannot be recognized in academic degrees received. It cannot be assessed by years of service. It cannot be weighed by public opinion surveys.

The only real measure of the worth of our accomplishments lies in the extent to which our efforts make a difference for the better in the lives of our fellow human beings.

—Appreciation Dinner Address, May 22, 1994.

What are the rewards that are meaningful? There is no point at which any of us can say we have it made. Life is a process—a struggle—and the meaning is in the process. Life should be an unfolding of new opportunities and new goals. So long as there are areas of injustice, human lives unused, physical ills unconquered, natural resources wasted, and corruption unchallenged, there will be meaningful work to do.

The greatest enemies we fight are those twin beasts— Apathy and Cynicism.

—Thoughts written on the back of an old envelope.

Strength lies in those qualities of compassion, tolerance, understanding, and love—an attitude that does not make conformity a necessary prerequisite to belonging.

—Thoughts written on a note card found in the personal papers in the William F. Winter Archives and History Building.

The greatest problem that we who live in the so-called "affluent society" have is to maintain a proper sense of balance in our attitude toward money—toward material possessions. As too many Americans learn to their sorrow, the acquisition of wealth is not a shortcut to happiness. It does not even guarantee security. Some of the most insecure men I know are men of comparatively large financial means, but they are forever worrying about what the future will bring for them.

Money, therefore, brings happiness only when it is held in consecrated stewardship or is given to God in a great and worthy cause. We can be loyal to ourselves in bringing joy and satisfaction into our lives only when we are wise stewards. It is not just a matter of benefitting God. God will get by. It is the benefit to the life and character of the giver that is worthy of our notice.

—Part of a speech written on a note card found in the personal papers in the William F. Winter Archives and History Building.

I think we tend to over-glamorize "happiness" as an end in itself. Happiness is a byproduct of constructive living that flows from work—even unpleasant work—well done. It is the result rather than the aim. And the greatest unhappiness most often comes to those who are most preoccupied with attaining happiness as a permanent and absolute state of living.

—"Mental Health and the Family," speech, 1960s.

ON RELIGION

In my almost twenty years of direct participation in political affairs I have seen and experienced many things that do not at first blush seem consistent with the ordinary patterns of worship. I have known and been fairly closely associated with all manner of gamblers, bootleggers, and petty crooks in the course of my political career. Many of them I think I can say in all candor were and are my friends. . . . I don't think any of us ought to feel as if by virtue of our work or our secular relation-ships we are automatically disqualified from knowing anything about the meaning of worship in our everyday lives. On the contrary, even though it may seem presumptuous to say it, I think maybe some of us who see a lot of the sordid, cynical side of life may be better qualified to talk on this subject than some pale, pious fellow who has spent his life in meditative retreat from the evils of the world.

The hardest thing that most of us have to do, though, is to maintain a consciousness of the relationship of what we do everyday to the pattern of worship that is set forth for us as Christians. This is not to say that we turn our back on our religion the minute we are outside the church. We all carry the church's work inside us even if it is reflected in nothing more than a guilt complex or a bad conscience. But too often for those who sincerely and earnestly try to do the right thing most of the time, there is not enough understanding on their part that in so doing they are engaging in an act of worship just as surely as and perhaps even more effectively than singing a hymn in church. Helping a neighbor in distress is as noble an act of worship as a man can perform, as Jesus showed in the story of the good Samaritan, and yet how few of us think of it in those terms.

But so obvious a comparison as that still does not go to the heart of this matter of extending the conscious experience of worship to our lives outside the direct influence of the church. How in short do we make everything we do relate to service to God? First of all we must understand that the purpose of all our work should always be directly or indirectly to serve God and man. And to a great extent it is our attitude toward our work that determines this rather than the specific kind of work that we do. It is how we do our work rather than what we do that ought to be our main concern.

. . . When more of us are able to see our job in terms of God's plan for our lives, it ceases to be just another job and becomes a means of contributing to His divine process.

The monks used to say, "To work is to pray." We are told that the dedicated craftsmen who helped to erect the magnificent medieval cathedrals worked just as painstakingly in the remote corners even though no one might ever see their work, because they worked "for God." Sometimes I wonder if we don't use the wrong approach when we just tell an intemperate cabinet-maker to lay off liquor. What we as churchmen ought to be telling him also is that the first demand of his religion is that he make good cabinets.

. . . One of the problems in our present status-seeking society is that we have set up a kind of hierarchy of jobs with different social levels attaching to different kinds of work. We have come to think of so-called white collar jobs as more satisfactory, although not necessarily more satisfying, than jobs involving manual labor. We have come to look on mental work as more creative than muscular work. And yet who would presume to say that the workman atop a power pole whose certain touch sends electric current coursing through the proper circuits into the executive's office is engaged in a work less creative or less vital simply because he wears a khaki shirt. And how could anyone believe that the seeming drudgery of the mother tending her small child as she helps mold his young life is engaged in anything less than a work of infinite creativity and an act of worship.

And at the same time that we tend to categorize work on a prestige basis, there is a further source of confusion as a result of the ambiguity of moral values. I think this is particularly true in the field of politics and to a lesser degree perhaps in business. But how often have I heard the exclamation of a sympathetic friend, "How can you possibly be a good Christian and a successful politician?" Well, in the first place I am not sure that either adjective is correct. But in any event it occurs to me that this query reveals an unreal conception of both Christianity and politics. There is implied here the idea that a Christian is a person who always does the right thing and that a politician or a businessman who, because he does not always do the right thing, cannot be a Christian. Obviously there are many situations when conflicts arise between what one's political or business commitment expects of him and what his Christian faith requires.

. . . Christ does not call us to be good men or pious men or religious men. He calls us to be His men. And we are never more worthy to be called His men than when we are engaged in proving our identity with Him in the reconciling work that must eternally go on out in the world. The Christian has no real opportunity to express his faith except as he does it in the area of his daily living. He must live with his face toward the world— with the church behind him to bolster him, to push him on, to be a base but not a goal. Our direction is a spreading outward from the church—not a withdrawing inward into the church.

At the same time this is the only way that the church can be strengthened. We don't attract those outside the church to come in by sitting around on our hands telling each other how good we all are. The quality of the lives of church members as reflected in what they do outside has always been one of the strongest bases on which God has drawn people to himself. This was abundantly demonstrated in the Book of Acts where the early church was able to expand in the face of unbelievable odds simply because other people could see in these early Christians a newness of approach to life that they wanted for themselves.

Let us latter-day Christians remember this. When we proclaim our Christianity but demonstrate no healing, when we talk about the great gift of God's love but don't show any love for each other; when we herald a great religion but show no signs of a new life, we make little impact on those outside our communion. In this connection let me say that I have attended meetings in our church and found less Christian understanding than I have seen in many a cynical political gathering.

—"Worship Through Work," speech, Fondren Presbyterian Church, Jackson, Mississippi, 1965.

For the manner in which a church meets its responsibility to witness for God has a great deal to say about the degree of freedom which it claims for itself. The very act of maintaining its freedom to witness to the lordship of Christ is a measure of how a church faces up to this obligation.

. . . The first job we have to do is to help unify mankind rather than to divide it. If we are going to render to God the effective service that He has a right to expect of us, we are going to have to do it together. We spend so much of our time splitting theological hairs—arguing about details of interpretation that 99 out of 100 of us really don't know or care anything about anyway—that we don't have time to get the Lord's work done.

. . . If we had spent as much of our time supporting our saints as we have in hunting heretics—if we had stood behind our ministers as much as we have stood in the way of them—if we had emphasized how much we agree with each other as how much we disagree, the Kingdom of Jesus Christ would be much farther advanced than it is today.

. . . Jesus said, "Love one another," and He intended no denominational nor geographical limits on his command. But he said more than that. He said not only are we to love one another, but we are to help one another. So here is another mission of the mature and responsible church. As Christians we must strive to see to it that we have the will and the energy to do the things that we must do not only to save our own souls but to save the world in which we live. We must know that it takes great tenacity of purpose and great courage to put into action the spirit of Christianity in a world that moves so often under the impact of base motives and ideas. The result too often of our realization that this is true is the development of a massive sense of negativism.

But it is not enough that we be against sin. We must be for the salvation of men—the salvation of men not only from their sinful lives but from the conditions that aided and abetted their sins—from ignorance and indignity and indolence. To accomplish this, we cannot do it just from a comfortable pew on Sunday morning.

. . . In the final analysis, the price of freedom along with the price of responsibility is one that can be paid only by the dedication of Christians possessed of those qualities of courage and conviction tempered by love and compassion and understanding. For in these troubled times it is frequently convenient to have scapegoats. A free and responsible church sometimes provides one for those who persist in sowing seeds of discord in the name of religion. But no church can long remain either free or responsible if it permits itself to be intimidated by those who would use it for man's purposes rather than for God's. This, therefore, is the challenge that rests on our shoulders—to see that a climate endures that will enable the church of Jesus Christ to be worthy of His name. This is a task that none of us may deem too small. This is a part of that eternal quest upon which we are embarked which will lead us in God's good time and by His grace into the radiant presence of "the Way, the Truth, and Life."

—"The Unity of the Church," speech, Fondren Presbyterian Church, Jackson, Mississippi, 1960s.

We live in a world created and ruled by a God who not only expects but demands that we act with boldness and imagination based on faith in His ultimate purpose. In circumscribing our lives with little thoughts, with petty schemes, with meaningless action, we not only sell ourselves short—we sell God short. God is working and he is working on no small scale. General William Booth was right when he said, "You can keep company with God only by running full speed."

And we cannot keep up if we are eternally concerned with our trivial little purposes—our personal prejudices based in so many cases on nothing that we can explain to our own satisfaction, let alone anybody else's—our narrow, man-enforced dogmatism that frequently makes a mockery of Christian love—our almost neurotic preoccupation with being against everything that we don't or won't understand—our vague and frantic quest for security at all costs.

We live in a world that now will not let us forget that just because we are white, Anglo-Saxon, English-speaking, anti-Communist Mississippians, we do not, in the casual language of the day "have it made." Let us be solemnly reminded that there are no guarantees that we are where we are simply because we have been so good and so smart. God does not operate that way. We are where we are because of His goodness and not ours. We enjoy the favored status that we have come to call the American way of life not because of anything that we have done—but because in the wonderful and mysterious pattern of God's eternal scheme of things we have had the good fortune to have been born into this good land. Did you ever ask yourself the sobering question: Why am I who I am rather than a starving peasant in China or a waif in a Latin American ghetto? And if this is not sobering enough, have you ever contemplated further the kind of responsibility that rests on you and me to try to justify this accident of birth?

—Commencement address, Belhaven College, Jackson, Mississippi, 1960s.

In our own little world of Mississippi we peer out and find a great many things happening that make us disturbed. We see a melancholy cloud of change hovering over our institutions and our way of life, and we feel threatened by it. We find ourselves swept unwillingly along an unknown way, and many of us are troubled and afraid.

. . . And understandably, in the face of all these issues and problems and changes, we find ourselves asking the haunting question: "Is nothing certain anymore?" And . . . all of us are caught up in this maelstrom of change, and we are all looking for some reassurance that this is the best of all possible worlds.

Maybe somebody made a mistake. Maybe we got put off on the wrong planet. "Stop this one and let me off!" we cry.

But before we all get crushed in the rush to push the panic button, let me pose the question that I think sensitive, intelligent Christian laymen ought to be asking. This is the question that I think puts in proper perspective our relationship to the troubled world in which we live.

That question . . . is simply this: "What is God's purpose for our lives in this world in which he has put us?" As contradictory as it seems, it is in confused times like these that we have the best opportunity to reflect upon and to understand God's purposes for us. This is so because there is so much to do—because there is so much that needs to be done. The first and obvious fact that tells us that we have a special role to play is the fact that in God's magnificent scheme of things he has seen fit to endow us with special privilege. By any standard you and I are the most privileged people on the face of the earth—in education, in economic affluence, in social standing, in opportunity for achievement and service. This fact of privilege then speaks too loudly to be ignored. And so it is the first measure of the basis of God's purpose for our lives.

There are people in this world—in Jackson and in Djakarta, on the Pearl and on the Po—who do not have the capacity or the understanding or the ability to help point the way. There are people so overwhelmed by ignorance or prejudice or hopelessness that they cannot handle their own lives much less anybody else's. But you and I have no such alibi, and the price of privilege is a social and political and religious responsibility that demands the highest and fullest use of all the talents that we have.

. . . You have a special duty to try to bring more unity and understanding to mankind and less division and alienation. There is no one of us who has such a monopoly on truth that we can stand on our little one square foot of earth and be assured of the eternal and everlasting righteousness of our position. So our job as twentieth-century Christians is to bring people together, not to divide them; to reconcile them, not to reject them. Our church, our nation, and our community will be served and saved only as enough of us echo the words of L. Q. C. Lamar in saying, "My countrymen, know one another and you will love one another."

. . . We must say to more in the bearing of our Christian witness that we are not Presbyterian against Catholic, or . . . that we are one kind of Presbyterian against another kind of Presbyterian; that we are not Democrat against Republican; that we are not Rebel against Yankee; that we are not white against Negro; but that we are Christians who are pledged to get along with one another and to treat one another as we would have the other treat us.

We can serve this cause of Christian citizenship another way, too, at a time when liberty is frequently confused with license. You and I who know better have a special obligation to uphold the law, for liberty without law is anarchy. When every man reserves a right to decide for himself which laws he will obey, the result is that the strong rule at the expense of the weak.

. . . This is the great difference between the society of which we are a part here in this country and societies in some of the more undeveloped areas of the world, or even in some of the more underprivileged areas of our own country. But just because there are people who would choose deliberate defiance of the law in their ignorance or their frustration or their anger, there is no excuse for any of us with the higher privilege of education and civic responsibility to be unmindful of our duty to uphold the law. Indeed, the more reckless and irresponsible that some of our fellow citizens may become in their disregard of the law, the greater is our duty to see to it that the law is respected and upheld.

As we view further our role from the vantage point of privilege, let us remember, too, that a free society can be a good society only as enough people assume the moral responsibility to meet the obligations of freedom. It means being willing to work for what we get. It means being concerned with putting more into society than we take out. It means looking for ways to serve rather than ways to be served.

. . . The price of privilege is reflected in another way. It means that we must be above the petty, cynical, vicious little attitudes that make a mockery of human dignity. In the name of Christian charity and common decency let us put away the sick, ridiculing jokes and stories whose effect is to hurt and demean any of God's people. Let us make certain that our sense of humor is based on a wholesome sense of values. It is a mark of privilege and maturity that we extend courtesy and thoughtfulness to all people, whoever they are and wherever they may be, whose lives may touch our own. We must remember to temper our conversations lest what we say be repeated with resultant misunderstanding and injury to another. You and I have a responsibility to act with patience and restraint toward others of less privilege, knowing that we must not expect too much in return but knowing, too, that no man is perfect, and that all of us must crawl before we walk and walk before we run. . . . We never know whose lives, whose attitudes, we may give shape to, but it is a solemn enough obligation to make us mindful at all times of the responsibility of our conduct and our conversations.

What I am simply suggesting is that each one of us who has been so greatly privileged must reject the shallowness and the conformity and the mediocrity that is suggested by the cheap little time-servers who would traffic in human weakness and frailty. Whenever any of us accepts a stature less than that of a free, sensitive human being, we become less than the person that God intended us to be. Some men have always used the fears of the unknown to force other men into a kind of herd conformity that is the sickness that could be the destroying agent of our free society. You and I must reject the exploitation of these fears and help others who might succumb to them to see more clearly what is required of them.

—Baccalaureate address, Fondren Presbyterian Church, Jackson, Mississippi, June 5, 1966.

There are so many people these days who seem to want to write off the traditional role of the minister as pastor and counselor of his people as now being irrelevant and unresponsive, and as a reaction to this popular attitude, I detect that many ministers . . . are turning to other more worldly fields of service.

I have talked to a great many people, in the church and out, young people and old people, highly educated and relatively uneducated, liberal and conservative, city people and rural people, and on the basis of what I have heard and sense and believe, I am persuaded that the greatest call for service today for the ministers of our church is not in the exotic far-out reaches of society or in some social action agency or in a narrowly specialized field of service, but that it is in the internal renewal of the religious community where we live—in the ministering in the name of Jesus Christ to the everyday spiritual needs of people.

Too many of our churches . . . all of the old main-line institutional churches have sometimes made the mistake of aligning themselves too closely by the side of secular social agencies and establishing for themselves no other identity than as another humanitarian calling doing good in one or many of the various areas of opportunity. I do not belittle the valuable special ministries that are being carried on in the name of the church in the fields of mental health and alcoholism and drugs and aging and all the rest. There is more to do in these great areas of social need than all of the agencies of government,

religion, and private enterprise put together can do. And this is
not to say that the church should not be greatly involved.

. . . The church cannot really be the church except as it is
committed to the formation and transmission of a basic system
of values out of which people act, react, and interact. The great
temptation for religion in other centuries, as in this, has been
the tendency to seek world favor and acceptance.

As a result there is . . . a growing suspicion of, if not actual
hostility to, religion and the church on the part of some people
who feel that too many who would speak for the church have
made an easy peace with the world.

Religion, particularly when it is observed as a mere adjunct
to the trappings of political power on a White House Sunday
morning or casually noted in the ceremonial prayers that open
a new shopping center or a football game, loses its capacity to
lead in direct proportion to the extent to which it lets itself
become just another institution in a highly pluralistic society.

And because you now become the professional spokesmen
for the church, I say to you that I hope you will regard this
newly acquired status as one which, without apology and without false pride, sets you apart to do a work that is more important than any other going on in the world. With the humility
that comes from the recognition of the sovereignty of God, you
now have the inescapable obligation to be His prophets.

As I say, this must be done without apology and with the
assurance that this is what is expected of you. There is no
greater disillusionment on the part of laymen about the ministry than that which is based on seeing some ministers who
would gain community acceptance by adopting the standards
of conduct and performance of the community as satisfactory
for themselves. This may win an easy entry into the best civic
clubs and social circles, but it wins no victories for the church,
and it is one of the prime reasons for the loss of respect for
religion.

What, therefore, can you do that will help to reestablish the preeminent place of religion in our society? First let me stress the need for you to go to the aid first of all of the people in the pews. As a layman, I can tell you that we are hoping for and looking to you to supply us with the kind of value system that will sustain us in our confrontations with the confusion and compromises of everyday living. I am tired of the cynicism and pessimism that I hear frequently from ministers in their attitude toward their ministry. It does appear so many times that nobody is listening, but . . . the reason that many appear not to listen is that they are not hearing that voice of prophecy which they have come expecting to hear. I tell you that you must not fall victim to that insidious, religion-destroying myth that average, middle-class, television-watching, run-of-the-mill people are unwilling to and will not respond to an appeal made in love for a set of values based on the hard discipline of sacrificial living. We have been getting too much sweet talk in the language of the street, and not enough straight talk in the words of Jesus Christ.

This is no time for the kind of theological timidity that I see so often when there are so many people waiting for you to give them the inspiration to raise their lives out of the malaise in which they find themselves living. And you cannot do it unless you are willing and able to point the way to the fulfillment that can come only out of self-denial and sacrifice that are at the heart of the Christian faith.

. . . Let me share with you also the insight, confused though it may be, of one who has been involved in the harsh world of secular politics for several years, but who at the same time has tried to have a meaningful part in the life of my church. There are some . . . who say that one cannot be both a successful politician and a proper churchman, and that may well be true. However, I would like to think that our political system, in spite of its Watergates and its other failings, has not become so base as to make it unworthy of the participation of Christian people, and by the same token, I would hope that our churches would not have become so pharisaical as to deny fellowship to those who have the dirt and grime of the political arena on their hands and faces.

. . . You, as ministers of the gospel of Jesus Christ, must be prepared to speak with the kind of prophetic insight that will help those of us who live in a world of cynicism and compromise to handle the hard decisions by giving us the ethical and moral understanding to know what to do and the courage to do it.

For God rules in the world of business and politics as everywhere else, and your task is to aid more of us to find the discipline to affirm that sovereignty of God in whatever we do. It is not enough, though, that from a lofty pulpit you merely condemn the double dealing and compromises and corruption of the political market place. In fact, all that this frequently does is to raise the level of self-righteousness of some pious people who, like the Pharisees of old, are so thankful that they are not engaged in such unreligious activity.

What is required is the insight and understanding that permits a politician or a businessman or anybody else, for that matter, in the face of a crisis of judgment or in a lapse of idealism to share with his minister . . . the anguish and uncertainty that come out of such experiences and, from such counsel, gain the renewal that enables one to find his place again. For we are all lost sheep, and, while you may reject the allegory, you are the shepherds. And the flock always includes some black sheep who have strayed off into places like the fields of politics and who need the sustaining voice that only you can give.

. . . I believe we are living today in a special testing time of the human spirit. There is a sense of lost-ness about our society today. Many of the political leaders that I know, with all of the wealth and power of state and nation at their disposal, speak despairingly of their sense of helplessness to chart a purposeful course.

. . . Out of this national malaise in which we find ourselves, we can lose our perspective and forget who we are and where we came from and where we are supposed to be going. We can succumb to the brute forces that have always walked this earth waiting for the weaknesses of mankind to give them their opportunity to overwhelm us. Your task is to stay those forces that gnaw at our vitals and remind us of the strength that abounds in the realization that we are all made in the image of Almighty God and that He has a divine purpose for each of us.

So many people don't believe that, and your task is to tell them and tell them in ways that they will hear and respond. Establishing a value system for our people based on this Christ-inspired concept of the worth and dignity of every individual is the only thing that will be effective in the face of the impersonal forces that threaten to deny us our identity and give us numbers instead of names.

You must not let us lose our personal identity, for when we cease to know each other as individuals and as brothers, then we really have lost our way. This is a high calling on which you have embarked, and only the divinely inspired can be worthy of it and effective in it. My special plea to you is that you never let any influence, whether it be the beguiling appeal of the comfortable life or the intimidating voices of those threatened by your cause or even the challenging pursuit of all manner of humanistic concerns, interfere with or compromise your unique role as God's own men bringing His prophetic message in what you do and how you live as well as by what you say.

Your great and compelling task in the final analysis is to help more of us to face life in these confused times bravely and unafraid.

—Commencement address, Columbia Theological Seminary, Decatur, Georgia, June 2, 1974.

I never have thought that God takes much stock in politics or makes a note of who's running for governor or president or what their platform is. He has given us some pretty good rules to live by. He has laid out the standards of how we ought to live our lives and how we ought to relate to each other. It is up to us to apply those rules in our daily conduct, whether it's in politics or business or anything else.

I believe that it is out of the inspiration of the teaching of Jesus that we have the basis for forming our own personal and political philosophy—and basic to that philosophy is the commitment to be engaged in the process of serving our communities and helping our fellow human beings—and especially those neighbors less fortunate than ourselves. Jesus told us that is what we ought to do. Politics is one way of doing that. It can be the most effective way of doing that.

—Speech, Grace Chapel Presbyterian Church, Madison, Mississippi, July 30, 2000.

I am deeply skeptical of those in politics who flaunt their religion in their political pursuits. I have seen my share of charlatans who have brazenly trafficked in religious rhetoric to further their own interests. Consequently I am reluctant to claim any special piety or grace in discussing my faith in a public way.

I do say, though, that in my eyes public service can be truly productive and meaningful and valuable only as it is guided by a value system that has its foundation in the ideals of one's religious faith. However, in the culturally and religiously diverse society of which we are a part, we have to be careful in seeking faith-based answers to complicated secular problems. There is a disturbing tendency in some circles these days to equate sectarian dogma with political ideology and suggest that God is allied with one political side or the other. That can make for a lot of trouble.

A better course I believe is simply to recognize that on most major public issues conscientious people of faith will hold a wide range of opinions. In approaching these issues we must remember that we live in a very diverse democracy—not a conforming theocracy. That is why we are called on to guard with special vigilance the concept of the separation of church and state.

. . . It seems to me that in these times when we are just about overwhelmed by the shrill and sensational images and messages of talk radio and the high-powered TV pulpit and the big movie screen, we could use a little peace and quiet as we try to figure it all out. This is when we have to fall back on that faith which can provide us not with specific answers to complicated questions but with an instinctive insight that leads us to a wise, fair, and compassionate sense of what is right.

It may best be summed up in the ultimate wisdom of that passage of scripture from the Book of Micah. "What does the Lord require of you but to do justice, and to love kindness, and to walk humbly with your God?" Following those directions just might lead us to where we need to go.

—"Reflections on a Life of Public Service," speech, Millsaps College, Jackson, Mississippi, March 9, 2004.

Over fifty years ago while still a student at the Ole Miss Law School I was elected to the Mississippi House of Representatives. It was a different and simpler time. We were less than a decade removed from the Great Depression and only two years removed from the end of World War II. All of us who entered politics for the first time that year were tempered by the harsh experiences of those two monumental events. I think it fair to say that as a result of that background we had a clearer understanding of the challenge and responsibility of public service, and we had a religious faith honed in the trials and tragedies of those difficult years of our youth.

Behind it all was also a recognition that public service would be productive and meaningful only as it was guided by a value system which relied on the basic tenets of one's religious faith. As a Christian who professed to believe in an all-powerful and all-loving God, I felt then as I feel now that religion ought to serve as a reconciling and healing force in our society— not as a divisive one.

That society is today more culturally and religiously diverse than it was when I first entered politics. This means that the choices we are confronted with in our public and private lives are more complex than they were in an earlier time. There is a disturbing tendency these days to try to reduce those choices to a naively simplistic approach represented by the question, "What would Jesus do?"

One of the dangers in that approach is that in our zeal to find religious answers to complicated secular problems we tend to equate sectarian dogma with political orthodoxy. That makes for a potent devil's brew.

A better course it seems to me is simply to recognize that on most major public issues conscientious and faithful Christians may hold deeply-felt differences of opinion.

. . . The point is that our Christian faith should provide us who are or have been public officials with the broad foundation on which to make wise, compassionate, and just decisions. There are so many times when the path is not clear cut. That is almost always the case when the issues are hotly contested. Then the conscientious official can only fall back on the instinctive insight that comes from his or her faith that creates a sense of what is right.

That faith, which I have tried to apply in my own life, has found special inspiration for me in many passages of scripture but from two in particular. The first is from the Book of Micah: "What does the Lord require of you but to do justice, and to love kindness, and to walk humbly with your God?" The other is the great commandment as set forth in the Gospel of Matthew: "As you did it to one of the least of these my brethren, you did it to me."

It seems to me if we strive to apply those standards to our daily living, whether it be in a political environment or not, we have the basis for making the right decisions. Following those guidelines, we are able to see our political adversaries in a different light.

Instead of trying to bash them into submission to our position we hopefully can find ways to resolve differences so as to produce positive results. There is too little of this kind of effort going on these days. This does not mean that we have to give up our commitment to our political beliefs and ideals. It ought to mean, though, that out of our religious faith we learn to respect and live in love with those who differ with us, however that difference may be manifested.

. . . The superficial differences based on what we look like or where we come from or how we dress or what we eat or how we worship soon pale into insignificance as we contemplate our responsibility to learn to know and serve and love one another. If somehow we could devote more of our public energy to the pursuit of that goal, then many of the problems that cause us so much grief and travail would disappear. If our faith means anything, it should mean our commitment to the realization of that ideal.

—"Faith and Politics," unpublished writings, 2004.

ON CHRISTMAS

But for most of us, wherever we have been on a particular Christmas, what is remembered most is the sense of belonging—of being a part of a thread of human existence that transcends physical distance and location and derives its meaning and its values from that divinely ordained event in a lowly and lonely Bethlehem stable 2000 Christmases ago. So as we pause to observe another Christmas in a world that has seen more than its share of pain these last twelve months, may we be sustained by the meaning of that first Christmas and by the acknowledgment of our common humanity that is shaped and tempered and ultimately transformed by our common divinity.

—Television commentary, WJTV, Jackson, Mississippi, 1985.

ON ATHLETICS

I do not believe that we do athletes a service when we let them get through school on athletic ability alone. Discipline is what is involved here, and an undisciplined student is apt to be an undisciplined athlete. I am persuaded that a good athlete will be a better athlete if he or she is required to maintain a satisfactory record in the classroom. Sports and scholarship can then both be served.

—Television commentary, WJTV, Jackson, Mississippi, 1985.

The thirties, with the dimension of radio as the principal ingredient, saw the emergence of larger than life figures into the consciousness of people living in the most remote rural areas. Franklin Roosevelt was the most commanding national political figure . . . but there were other notable figures that commanded my attention as well. Many were athletes.

During the World Series time before we had a radio the public square in Grenada was equipped with a primitive loud speaker that blared out the play-by-play exploits of my faraway heroes. I was as fascinated by their names as by their performance—Schoolboy Rowe and Goose Goslin of the Tigers, Dizzy Dean and Pepper Martin of St. Louis. I felt as if I knew them all. I memorized their averages. Cool Papa Bell, who some later said may have been the best ball player that had ever come out of Mississippi up to that time, was not among them. Cool Papa was black.

But there was one black athlete that we did know about. No figure so captured the imagination of the black South in that period as Joe Louis. As his fame as a fighter grew, his picture would be found over the fireplace in most of the grimy little tenant houses on the farm. Babies were named for him. Young black boys could be seen shadowboxing along the paths to the cotton fields. In the cool of summer evenings the tenants would gather on the grass outside our bedroom window to listen to the broadcasts of Louis's fights on our radio. I remember hearing some of them quietly sobbing the night that the German, Max Schmeling, knocked him out. Louis, who had come off an Alabama farm himself, was one of the few heroes they had.

—Unpublished personal memoirs.

A few weeks ago in between my teaching assignments at the Harvard School of Government, I ventured out to see the local Boston Red Sox play the White Sox from Chicago. What makes this reportable to a Mississippi audience is that the winner of that game and something of a folk hero in New England was Oil Can Boyd of Meridian, Mississippi, and Jackson State University. It did this displaced Mississippian's heart good to watch those New England Yankees with their unique Boston accents stand up in the late innings and cheer that Southerner's every pitch. "Oil Can! Oil Can! Oil Can!" they would shout in unison. It was a heartening coming together of Americans united in nothing more profound than an appreciation of the capacity of a young black man to play an American game about as well as it could be played.

—Television commentary, WJTV, Jackson, Mississippi, 1985.

Whatever the past year may have brought to Mississippi, and all the news wasn't cheerful, there was one individual who continued to reflect special credit on his home state. I refer to that incredibly gifted and motivated young man from Marion County by way of Jackson State University and the Chicago Bears—"Sweetness" himself—Walter Payton. Not only has he established himself as the finest running back ever to play the game of football, but at a time when there are a lot of heroes with clay feet he has emerged as a role model for us all. I remember the first time I ever saw him. It was a late afternoon scrimmage on the old practice field at Jackson State in the early 1970s. Even then in that unpretentious setting there was a quality about this remarkable young man that stamped him as a natural leader and a future superstar. What has set him apart from many other gifted athletes has been his insistence on giving his best all of the time—whether carrying a football or blocking for someone else or setting an example for others to follow. Regardless of how much recognition he may have achieved or what honors have come his way, he has remained the same self-confident but unspoiled and modest individual that many of us first knew fifteen years ago.

—Television commentary, WJTV, Jackson, Mississippi, 1985.

ON PETS

While we were living at the Governor's Mansion we acquired a little schnauzer dog that we called Toby. He came to be one of the best known members of our household and was even the subject of comment by the news media from time to time. While he was not exactly a publicity hound, he did insist on coming to my press conferences. I tried to discourage his presence at staff meetings lest there be reports that my administration was going to the dogs. Still Toby probably influenced public policy more than I knew about. For instance, I never learned what damage may have resulted after he mistook a member of the legislature for a fireplug.

—Television commentary, WJTV, Jackson, Mississippi, 1985.

As a boy growing up on a farm . . . I was more interested in pigs and goats [than cattle]. . . . My special pet pig was a light-colored animal whom I named Sandy Sanford after a University of Alabama football player whose two game-winning field goals that fall had put the Crimson Tide into the Rose Bowl. He became my momentary athletic hero. Sandy, the pig, would often follow me to the school bus stop. That was as far as he was permitted to go, although I felt that he would have been welcomed by my classmates. But the goat went to school one day. It was in response to a call for a bit part in the senior play. They needed a goat as a walk-on character, and I volunteered Maggie for the role. She and I rode the bus together. I tied her to the see-saws outside the school building while I went to class. As I recall, she performed brilliantly that evening. Unfortunately, she never got another call, and a few weeks later her promising stage career was ended forever when one of my father's mules delivered a fatal kick to the head of the little goat.

—Unpublished personal memoirs.

ON FAMILIES

Our form of government, based as it is on the concept of the worth of the individual, cannot survive unless there is a strong family life where ideals are learned and developed, where fundamental truths are instilled, where discipline and responsibility are experienced, where only preparation for individual citizenship can be had. The kind of country that we have in the next generation will be directly related to the kind of family life we have in this one.

We talk much of the threat of Communism to this country, and we grope around about how we can do something about it. Let me tell you that there is no more effective deterrent that we can provide to stem the menace of Communism than the maintenance of strong family relationships in this country. If our family life breaks up, our country breaks up. It is, I think, as simple as that.

—"Mental Health and the Family," speech, 1960s.

A fact of life that must be of concern to all thoughtful people of whatever political persuasion is the continuing disintegration of the structure of the American family. A high proportion of single parent families . . . will be poor people. The results have tragic implications for the children born into this environment. We have now become the first society in history where children as an age group have the highest incidence of poverty. This has special meaning for those of us who live in the South. Not only do we have the highest percentage of children in our population, but we have by far the highest percentage of poor children. This is a problem that cannot be left to ivy-towered sociologists to talk about. It presents a challenge to all responsible citizens to solve. If we do not, the costs in domestic tranquility and economic stability will be high in the years ahead.

—Television commentary, WJTV, Jackson, Mississippi, 1985.

Most of us parents and especially us fathers start out having to learn so much about our children. In fact, we soon come face to face with the reality that we really don't know very much about anything and that, as Leo Rosten once wrote, "we never really grow up; we just grow taller." So much of my learning from my children occurred as we all grew taller together.

It is that recognition that we must learn from each other—from different perspectives but from shared experiences—that enables us to find the common thread that overcomes generational differences. I had learned that in growing up with my own father who, in spite of more than fifty years separating our births, considered me his own age. As a six-year-old boy, I shall never forget how on a bitter winter evening in our farm home he called me to his bedside. Desperately ill with pneumonia and with the corpse of his own father lying in an open casket in another room, he pressed me to his side and said, "Son, if I don't make it, you take care of mama." My father recovered from that illness, but I understood forever afterward how fragile and yet how binding the links of family can be.

Most of what I have learned from my own children has come from our learning together. It has been through those shared experiences that we have learned about each other and of what we expected from each other and of what we were willing to do for each other. And it has been in the hard times that we have probably learned the most.

"My Family," speech, Renaissance Meeting, Hilton Head Island, South Carolina, 1993.

ON WHAT I WOULD TELL MY GRANDSON

If he were here and if he were listening, I think I would say some things like this. . . . We can't know much about who we are unless we have an understanding of where we have come from. We have to remember that we are not just isolated individual beings who happen to occupy a few cubic feet of space on this planet for a brief period of time. Each of us is a continuing living part of a stream of people—some noble and notable—some weak and wanting—who for better or for worse have put a certain stamp on us.

. . . I would, in short, impress on him the significance of the incredible human tapestry of which he finds himself a part—of the warp and woof of talent and temperament, of gloom and glory, of happiness and hurting, of life and death that already form the patterns and shape of his young life. I would try to tell him that he will be adding to that tapestry, and that he can make it richer and brighter or, on the other hand, he can flaw it and scar it. I would have him understand that that choice will be up to him but the effects of his choice will not be his alone.

It is important . . . for this little boy to know that the world does not begin nor end with him and that in between his being born and his dying, he has a link to forge.

I would tell him, as William Faulkner told his daughter's graduating class at Oxford High School many years ago, that he must never be afraid—that, as Faulkner said, he must never be afraid to raise his voice for honesty and truth and compassion, against injustice and lying and greed and if he is afraid, to go on and do it anyway. And, more than that, I would counsel him that he also must not be afraid to fail. I would try to impress on him that he must be willing to take chances and defy risks, that he must stretch himself at times to limits that may exceed his grasp but that in the stretching he will add to his strength and resiliency. I would tell him to be himself, to be willing to follow his own instincts, to sail against the wind, to set a course uninfluenced by the easy standards and conventions of society. He must understand that life is not a voyage for the short-winded or the faint-hearted, that there are mighty few easy victories and that even those he wins will not ensure lasting contentment and satisfaction.

I would remind him that throughout his existence on this planet there will be an endless continuation of the experiences that have already marked his young life—of falling down and getting back up—sometimes with a bruise or two—but always getting back up to face with aplomb and good humor whatever life may have to offer. For of all the qualities that come closest to ensuring one's success, none is more vital than persistence.

I would try somehow to tell him that he will be living in a world full of diverse human beings and that he must learn how to get along with other people, especially those whose culture and background and religion and color are different from his own. I would hope that he would learn how to lead but also how to serve. I would want him to be a conservative in the assertion of his own rights, but I would want him to be a liberal in the extension of those same rights to others. In short, I would teach him, if I could, how to live with the confidence and self-assurance and compassion that are the true measure of a mature man or woman.

Finally, I would tell him that he must learn to laugh—at himself first of all and at much of the contradictory and ridiculous that he will find around him. I would hope that he would learn to be serious in the application of his talents but that he would at the same time not take himself so seriously as to lose sight of the simple pleasures that come from the associations of family and friends. For I would want him most of all to remember that he will always be sustained, wherever he may go or whatever he may do, by the love and devotion of those of us whose heritage and name he bears.

—"What I Would Tell My Grandson," speech, Hilton Head Island, South Carolina, December 30, 1988.

ACKNOWLEDGMENTS

This publication is made possible by generous contributions to the University of Mississippi Foundation from the following:

Dr. Tim and Mary Al Alford
Eleanor Winter and Daniel Backo
Dick and Mickee Boyd
Cecil and Nancy Brown
In loving memory of Travis Taylor Brown by Janet H. Brown
Tom and Terri Burnham
Harold Burson
The Crews Family—June, John, Billy, Catherine, David, and
    Claire
Danny and Sharon Cupit
Charles M. and Mary Dent Deaton
Kane and Betsy Ditto
Robb and Virginia Farr
Brian and Kelly Fenelon
Ken and Mary Foose
David and Sunny Fowler
William C. Gartin, Jr.
Guy and LeLe Gillespie
Vaughn and Sandy Grisham
John and Morella Henegan
Hinds Community College Development Foundation

Charles Holder
Richard and Lisa Howorth
Journal Publishing Company
Chancellor Robert C. Khayat
Guy Paul Land
Rabbi Seth Limmer
Daniel Logan and John Lovorn—The PACE Group
MDC, Inc.
Jerry and Sue McBride
Dr. and Mrs. S.H. McDonnieal, Jr.
Jean and Tim Medley
Dick and Sally Molpus
Alan L. Moore
Mark Musick
Jere Nash
Charles L. Overby
John N. Palmer
George and Carol Penick
Jack R. Reed, Sr.
Stephen and Harriet Roberts
Sally Robinson–MDC Member
Dr. and Mrs. George Schimmel
Jane and Tom Wacaster
John A. Waits
Jane and Tommy Walman
Watkins Ludlam Winter & Stennis, P.A.
Blake and Ann Wilson
Anne V. Winter

I want to thank Governor Winter's personal secretary, Debbie Nalley, for her able assistance. Debbie greeted with good humor and patience my constant requests to look through another filing cabinet and to make numerous copies of the contents. A special thanks also should go to Anne Stascavage at University Press for her assistance and suggestions.